New CLAIT 2006

Unit 1
File Management and e-Document Production

Using
Microsoft® Windows 7 & Word 2007

Release NC646v1

Published by:

> CiA Training Ltd
> Business & Innovation Centre
> Sunderland Enterprise Park
> Sunderland SR5 2TH
> United Kingdom

> Tel: +44 (0)191 549 5002
> Fax: +44 (0)191 549 9005

> E-mail: info@ciatraining.co.uk
> Web: www.ciatraining.co.uk

ISBN 13: 978-1-86005-848-6

Important Note

This guide was written using *Windows 7* with a screen resolution of 1024 x 768.

Using Windows XP will result in many dialog boxes looking different, although the content is the same.

Working in a different screen resolution, or with an application window which is not maximised, will change the look of the *Office 2007* Ribbon. The ribbon appearance is dynamic, it changes to fit the space available. The full ribbon may show a group containing several options, but if space is restricted it may show a single button that you need to click to see the same options, e.g. the **Editing**

group may be replaced by the **Editing** button .

First published 2010

Copyright © 2010 CiA Training Ltd

CIA Training's guides for **New CLAIT 2006** are a collection of structured exercises to provide support for each unit in the new qualification. The exercises build into a complete open learning package covering the entire syllabus, to teach how to use a particular software application. They are designed to take the user through the features to enhance, fulfil and instil confidence in the product. The accompanying data enables the user to practise new techniques without the need for data entry.

UNIT 1: FILE MANAGEMENT AND E-DOCUMENT PRODUCTION - The guide supporting this core unit contains exercises covering the following topics:

• Main Parts of a Computer	• Opening Files
• Health and Safety	• Editing and Printing Documents
• Using the Ribbon	• Formatting Documents
• Creating Files/Folders	• Document Security
• Moving & Copying Files/ Folders	• Selecting and Moving Text
• Using the Mouse and Keyboard	• Changing Alignment and Line Spacing
• Working with Windows	• Margins
• Shutting Down the Computer	• Creating Simple Tables
• Data Entry	• Applying Borders and Shading
• Saving Work	• Searching
• Cursor and Mouse Movement	• Spelling/Grammar Checker

Visit **www.ciasupport.co.uk** for hints, tips and supplementary information on published CiA products.

This guide is suitable for:

- Any individual wishing to sit the OCR examination for this unit. The user works through the guide from start to finish.

- Tutor led groups as reinforcement material. It can be used as and when necessary.

Aims and Objectives

To provide the knowledge and techniques necessary for the attainment of a certificate in this core unit. After completing the guide the user will be able to:

- Start and Shut Down the Computer, and recognise the Desktop and Mouse Pointers

- Manipulate Windows and Screens

- Work with Files and Folders

- Understand Health and Safety and Security Issues

- Create, Save, Edit, Format and Print Documents

Downloading the Data Files

The data associated with these exercises must be downloaded from our website. Go to: **www.ciatraining.co.uk/data**. Follow the on screen instructions to download the appropriate data files.

By default, the data files will be downloaded to **CIA DATA FILES\New CLAIT 2006\Unit 1 Windows 7 Data** in the **Documents** library.

If you prefer, the data can be supplied on CD at an additional cost. Contact the Sales team at **info@ciatraining.co.uk**.

Introduction

This guide was created using *Windows 7* and *Word 2007*. It assumes that the programs have been correctly and **fully** installed on your personal computer. Some features described in this guide may not work if the program was not **fully** installed. The business versions of *Windows 7* have a hierarchical system of users. Each user is given a particular status that governs what they can and cannot do. The types of user are: **Administrators, Power Users, Restricted Users**.

Notation Used Throughout This Guide

- Key presses are included within < > e.g. **<Enter>** means press the Enter key.

- Occasionally, choices to be selected are written, e.g. **Page Layout | Orientation** means select the **Page Layout** tab from the **Ribbon** and then click the **Orientation** button.

- The guide is split into individual exercises. Each exercise consists of a written explanation of the feature, followed by a stepped exercise. Read the **Guidelines** and then follow the **Actions**, with reference to the **Guidelines** if necessary.

Recommendations

- Work through the exercises in sequence so that one feature is understood before moving on to the next.

- Read the whole of each exercise before starting to work through it. This ensures the understanding of the topic and prevents unnecessary mistakes.

Assessment of Knowledge

At the end of this guide is a section called the Record of Achievement Matrix. Before the guide is started it is recommended that the user complete the matrix to measure the level of current knowledge.

Tick boxes are provided for each feature. 1 is for no knowledge, 2 some knowledge and 3 is for competent.

After working through a section, complete the Record of Achievement matrix for that section and only when competent in all areas move on to the next section.

Section 1

Fundamentals

By the end of this Section you should be able to:

Recognise the Main Parts of a Computer

Log on with a Password

Appreciate Health and Safety Issues

Recognise the *Windows* Desktop

Use the Mouse

Recognise Mouse Pointers

Use the Taskbar and Start Menu

Shut Down and Restart a Computer

Exercise 1 - Introduction to your Computer

Guidelines:

A computer can be terrifying; it's a fact - especially when you don't even know how to switch it on. However, once you get to know them, computers can be fun to use and can make your life much easier. More good news: unless you throw a computer around, it's almost impossible to break it and it's actually quite easy to correct any mistakes you may make!

This exercise will help you to become familiar with the different parts of a computer.

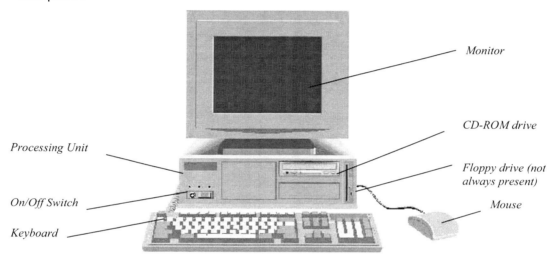

An alternative computer layout is shown on the next page - yours may look similar to either one.

Actions:

1. Use the diagram above to identify the **keyboard**. This is used to type (input) information.

2. Now find the **monitor** or Visual Display Unit (**VDU**), which is used to view information entered into the computer. It looks like a television screen.

3. Locate the **mouse**, which gets its name from the "tail" (wire) that attaches it to the computer (your mouse may not have a "tail" if it is a wireless mouse). It is usually located on a small portable pad called a **mouse mat**.

4. When you move the mouse about on its mouse mat, a cursor, moves in the same direction on the monitor. The mouse enables you to select options shown on the screen. Later exercises will teach you how to do this.

5. The **processing unit**, a big box, usually found either underneath or to one side of the monitor, or even underneath the desk, contains the "brains" - microchips, etc. - and wiring which allow the whole thing to work. This is the most important part of the system. The **Hard Disk Drive**, which is used to store programs and data, is found inside this box.

continued over

Exercise 1 - Continued

This type of computer is called a "tower" system

6. Find the **floppy disk drive**. It may look like the one in either of the two diagrams, lying horizontally, or turned sideways, but will have a little button (used to eject disks) next to it. This drive allows you to insert a floppy disk, so that you can transfer work to and from the computer, should you need to.

Note: *Find out how to insert a floppy disk on the computer you are using. This can vary from machine to machine, as floppy disk drives are not always installed in the same direction. Some computers do not have a floppy disk drive at all.*

7. Most computers also have a **CD-ROM drive** to read information from a compact disk (CD), which can contain software, information or music. Try to find this drive on your computer.

Note: *To insert a CD, press the **Eject** button, , to open the drive. Place the CD label side up into the "drawer" and then press the same button to close the drive.*

8. Your computer may have **speakers** attached, to play music or listen to communications. Can you find any speakers? They may be part of the computer rather than separate from it.

9. Make sure you know where all these parts are on the computer you are using. They are known as **hardware**. Computer **software** consists of the programs that allow you to use the computer, such as the operating system (*Windows*), games, word processor or spreadsheet application/program. <u>You can touch hardware but not software.</u>

Exercise 2 - Health and Safety

Guidelines:

A workplace that has swivel chairs with adjustable positions, stable, roomy desks, etc. will provide a working environment that is comfortable and safe. Furniture and equipment should be suitably positioned and conform to the relevant Health and Safety at Work (HASAW) legislation. Injuries common in an IT environment are:

- Aches and pains due to bad posture when seated for long periods

- Repetitive strain injury (RSI) caused by poor position of the seat/desk combined with repeated movements of the same joints over a long period of time

- Paper cuts from refilling printers/photocopiers

- Eye strain which can be caused by glare or flickering from a VDU and by not taking regular visual breaks (10 minutes every hour is recommended) away from the screen

- Electric shocks due to incorrect working practice or dangerous wiring

- Injuries due to tripping over trailing wires or other obstructions.

There should be:

- Provision of adequate lighting and ventilation

- VDUs appropriately positioned with screens free from flicker and interference and images free from glare

- Provision of blinds to minimise direct sunlight

- Sufficient legroom and desk space to allow you to move around

- Suitable desktop space

- A suitable, adjustable chair to provide safe and comfortable posture for the user.

Actions:

1. Make sure your chair is at the correct height and angle so that you can sit comfortably at the computer. Your feet should be flat on the floor and your back should be straight.

2. Make sure that you can see the screen properly and that there is no glare. You can change the angle of the monitor if necessary.

3. When you are entirely comfortable, move on to the next exercise.

Exercise 3 - Security

Guidelines:

Usually today, most computers have protection against unauthorised access by requesting a log in name (**user name**) and password. You may have to log on to the computer you are using now. Occasionally, it may be necessary to change your password; you can do this be pressing <**Ctrl Alt Delete**> and selecting **Change a password**. Type your current password and then your new password.

Note: It may be necessary on some networks to ask the IT Administrator to do this for you.

It is also very sensible to have some form of virus protection on a computer, especially if it is used to send and receive e-mail. Some viruses operate by infecting a file as soon as it is opened, then causing the file to automatically save to disk, carrying the virus with it.

Sometimes, it may be necessary to protect a file itself. It is possible to prevent a file from being opened by an unauthorised person by applying a password to it. This means that unless you know the password, you cannot open the file. This may be necessary for files that contain sensitive or personal information, such as payroll details for example.

Exercise 4 - Logging On

Guidelines

As mentioned in the previous Exercise, many computers will require that you log on using a password.

Actions:

1.   Switch the computer on.

2.   *Windows 7* allows more than one user to sign on to the same computer and maintain their own profile. The welcome screen shows icons for every available user defined on this computer and allows the correct profile to be selected. The screen is displayed even if there is only one user account available.

3.   Click your user name or icon to start *Windows* with your profile active.

continued over

Exercise 4 - Continued

4. If your account is password protected, you will be prompted for the password now. If you are connected to a network you may be prompted for a different **User name** and **Password**.

5. The *Windows* **Desktop** screen is displayed.

6. The **Desktop** screen can be personalised and therefore look quite different to the picture here. Usually the main features will consist of a background image, a number of small images (icons) arranged in columns and a bar along the bottom of the screen containing further icons (Taskbar). These features will be described in the following exercises.

Note: *You may need some help logging on, if you have never used the keyboard or mouse before. The next exercises will help you, but ask someone to show you what to do to at this stage.*

Exercise 5 - The Windows Desktop

Guidelines:

Windows uses a **Graphical User Interface** (**GUI**), which is a way of showing the computer's facilities using **icons** (pictures) and **menus** (names). Instead of typing a technical instruction, the mouse is used to click on an icon (picture) or menu (name) to select or perform an action. You can see these icons on the **Desktop**. The way the **Desktop** looks can be changed to suit the computer user: For this reason, *the screens shown in this guide may not quite match that of your computer*. Don't worry, because the basic layout should be the same.

Actions:

1. The screen shows the **Desktop**. This is the work area for all tasks performed in *Windows*. From here it is possible to access all the programs on the computer, manage how it works and use all the features of *Windows*.

2. The screen is similar to that shown below. Your screen may have a different background and have more or fewer icons.

Desktop Icons — *Gadgets (may not be prese...)* — *Taskbar* — *Start Button*

3. The **Desktop** is divided into two parts. Along the bottom of the screen is a bar known as the **Taskbar**. This is used as a quick way to access certain features. This bar usually remains on screen at all times. The remainder of the **Desktop** is taken up by **icons** (small pictures with text).

4. These icons represent programs saved on the **Desktop** or shortcuts that lead directly to a program, folder, file, etc. They will be used later. Gadgets are small informational programs which can be added to the **Desktop**, usually at the right edge.

Exercise 6 - The Mouse: Holding and Moving

Guidelines:

The mouse lets the computer know what you want it to do. It is worth taking the time to learn how to hold and move the mouse properly, although it can take a while to get used to it.

Actions:

1. If you have a mouse mat, make sure the mouse is on it. This prevents the mouse slipping when it is being used. If there is no mouse mat, a sheet of paper will do.

2. If you are right handed, the mouse should be at the right of the computer and for those who are left handed it should be on the left.

3. Make sure the "tail" of the mouse is pointing away from you and rest your hand on the mouse, as in the diagram below.

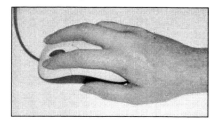

4. If you are right handed your thumb should rest at the left of the mouse and the base of the mouse should fit snugly into the palm of your hand. Left handed users will need to position the mouse accordingly.

5. Rest your fingers over the buttons, but do not press them. If the mouse has three buttons, ignore the one in the centre. Only the left and right buttons are to be used.

Note: Some mice have a central wheel that is used for scrolling through documents.

6. When the mouse feels comfortable, slowly move it around on the mat and watch what happens on the screen. The mouse pointer, should mirror the movements you make with your hand.

7. Move the mouse up and away from you. The pointer moves up the screen.

8. Now move the mouse toward you to make the pointer move down the screen.

Note: Don't worry if the pointer seems to disappear from view. Just move the mouse around the mat slowly until the pointer becomes visible again.

9. Practise moving the mouse around until you are able to control it and make it go where you want.

Exercise 7 - The Mouse: Clicking

Guidelines:

Nearly all *Windows* tasks can be performed using the mouse. There are a few different mouse techniques, they are:

Point *position the mouse pointer until the tip of the pointer on the screen rests on the required position*

Click *press and immediately release the left mouse button without moving the mouse*

Double click *click the left mouse button twice in rapid succession*

Right click *click with the right button of the mouse*

Note: *Both the left and right mouse buttons are used to perform tasks in Windows, <u>unless stated, use the left mouse button</u>.*

Actions:

1. Move the mouse pointer over the **Computer** icon on the screen. Holding the mouse steady, click once on the icon. It becomes highlighted to show that it has been **selected**.

2. Move the mouse pointer to a clear part of the **Desktop** and click to **deselect** the icon.

3. In *Windows*, one click nearly always selects an item. Double clicking does something different. Move the mouse over **Computer** again.

4. Hold the mouse steady and quickly click twice on the icon. If you have managed to double click correctly you should now be able to see a **window** (box) open on the **Desktop**. This is the **Computer** window.

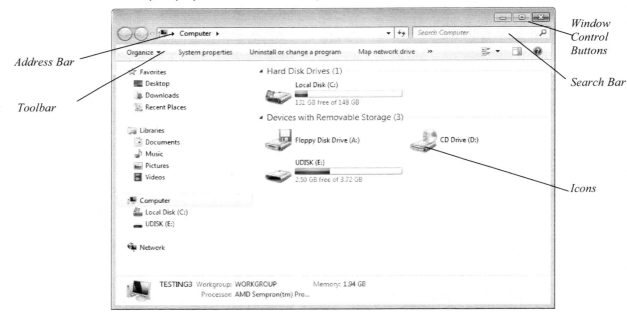

continued over

Exercise 7 - Continued

5. If the window fills the screen click once on the **Restore Down** button, 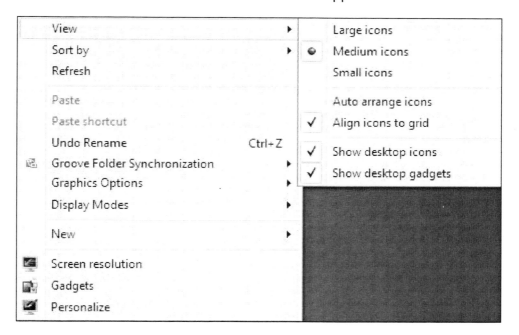, at the top right of the screen.

6. If the window is not visible, just click once on a blank part of the screen, then try again to double click on the **Computer** icon. You will need to click quickly.

7. **Windows** are dealt with a little later. For now, the **Computer** window needs to be closed. At the top right corner of the window there is a small orange button with a cross, [X]. Move the cursor over the button and notice the **Screen Tip**, **Close**. Click once to close the window.

8. Now try right clicking. Move the mouse pointer over a blank part of the **Desktop** and click once with the right mouse button. A **shortcut menu** is displayed.

9. Place the cursor over **View** and a further menu appears.

View	►	Large icons
Sort by	►	⦿ Medium icons
Refresh		Small icons
Paste		Auto arrange icons
Paste shortcut		✓ Align icons to grid
Undo Rename	Ctrl+Z	✓ Show desktop icons
Groove Folder Synchronization	►	✓ Show desktop gadgets
Graphics Options	►	
Display Modes	►	
New	►	
Screen resolution		
Gadgets		
Personalize		

10. If **Auto Arrange icons** has a tick at its left (to show this option is currently selected), then click on the words **Auto arrange icons** to turn it off ready for the next exercise when you will learn how to click and drag.

Note: **Auto arrange icons** keeps the icons in place on the left, they cannot be moved.

11. If the menus are still on screen, click once on a blank area of the screen to remove them.

Exercise 8 - The Mouse: Dragging

Guidelines:

The mouse can be used to move items around the screen, to make them bigger or smaller and to select areas. The technique used to do this is known as **click and drag**.

Actions

1. With **Auto Arrange icons** turned off, the icons on the **Desktop** can be moved about. Click on any icon and <u>hold the mouse button down</u>.

2. Drag the icon around the screen by moving the mouse.

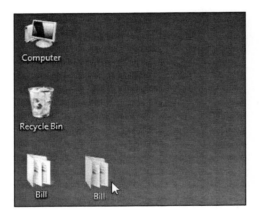

3. Release the mouse button to place the icon at the new position.

4. Use the same technique to move the icon back to its original position.

5. By clicking and dragging, move some of the icons about the **Desktop**.

6. Right click on a blank part of the screen to display the shortcut menu and move the cursor over the **View** option to display another list of options.

7. If the **Align icons to grid** option does not have a tick next to it, i.e. it is not set on, click once with the left mouse button to set it. This option ensures the icons are kept in the same order but automatically spaced.

8. Click with the right mouse button again, select **Sort by** and then by **Name**. The icons on the **Desktop** are now arranged neatly, in alphabetical order by name.

9. Click with the right mouse button again and select **Sort by | Size**. The icons are now arranged with the largest file first.

10. Rearrange the icons by **Name** again. A little later you will practise click and drag some more.

Exercise 9 - Mouse Pointers

Guidelines:

Windows uses several different types of mouse pointer. Until now you have probably just seen the arrow pointer, ⬉, but there are a few more that it may be useful to recognise. The type of pointer can give clues about what the computer is doing.

Actions:

1. Try to familiarise yourself with the following pointers, which you will probably come across sooner or later:

Pointer	Name	Meaning
⬉	**Arrow**	used to select options, to click on things
◯ or ⬉	**Busy**	this shows the computer is thinking about something. Don't panic and don't try to do anything until this pointer disappears. The computer will not do anything else until it is ready
I	**I-beam**	appears on a text document when the mouse is over the typing area, so you can easily click to place it between letters
✛	**Move**	used to move pictures or objects around a page
↕, ⬌, ⬉ or ⬈	**Resize**	changes depending on where it is placed and can be diagonal, vertical or horizontal
👆	**Link Select**	this pointer is displayed when a link to another location is available. Click the mouse to go to the linked destination
+	**Crosshair**	used to select areas of pictures, or to draw shapes
⊘	**Unavailable**	appears when you are trying to access an unavailable option.

Exercise 10 - The Taskbar

Guidelines:

The **Taskbar** is displayed across the bottom of the screen. The **Start** button is on the left, a notification area is on the right, and some of the remaining bar contains icons. These represent shortcuts to selected tasks which have been placed (pinned) there, and icons for tasks that are currently running.

More than one program may run at the same time (multi-tasking). As each program is started, an icon for it appears on the **Taskbar**. The icons for active programs have a light background, the currently selected program is lighter.

Actions:

1. Look at the left half of the **Taskbar**.

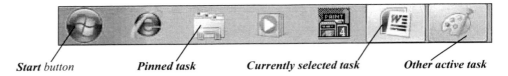

Start button   *Pinned task*   *Currently selected task*   *Other active task*

Note: *This is the default view of the **Taskbar** showing some pinned tasks and some active tasks. Different settings will show the active tasks in more detail, e.g.*

2. Hold the mouse pointer over each of the short cut icons on the **Taskbar**. After a few seconds a **ToolTip** is displayed with the program description.

Note: *If the pointer is held over an active task icon on the **Taskbar**, more detailed **information** is displayed including the name of any files open within the application.*

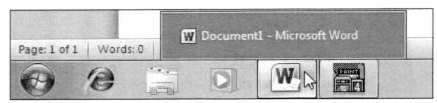

3. The right of the **Taskbar** is the **Notification** area. This contains settings which give information or can be changed, such as the date and time.

continued over

Exercise 10 - Continued

4. Right click on any of the non active icons on the left of the **Taskbar**. Notice that there is an option to **Unpin this program from taskbar**. This is how task icons are removed from the **Taskbar**. Do not select the option.

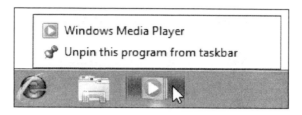

Note: *Right clicking on a program in any other position, e.g. the **Start** menu, will give the option to **Pin to Taskbar**. This is how program task icons are added to the **Taskbar**.*

5. Point at any unoccupied area of the **Taskbar** and right click. If there is a tick to the left of the **Lock the taskbar**, click on the words **Lock the taskbar** to turn off this setting off.

6. Point to any unoccupied area on the **Taskbar**. Click and drag to the right of the screen, to move the **Taskbar**. The **Taskbar** can be placed at any edge of the screen.

7. Move the **Taskbar** back to the bottom.

8. Move the mouse pointer slowly over the top of the **Taskbar**. The mouse pointer will change shape into a double-headed arrow. This **Resize** pointer changes the size of the **Taskbar**.

9. Click and drag up slightly to double the size of the **Taskbar**.

10. While the **Resize** pointer is visible, click and drag down to reduce the **Taskbar** to its default size, i.e. one line.

11. Right click on the **Taskbar** and click **Lock the taskbar** to fix it again.

Exercise 11 - The Start Menu

Guidelines:

At the left of the **Taskbar**, is the **Start** button, . This button is used to start any program that is loaded on the computer and has been included in the menus.

Actions:

1.   Click the **Start** button to display the **Start** menu.

2.   The contents of this menu may be different depending on how your computer has been set up. The normal **Start** menu options at the right are:

        Your named folder   *your own folder, with access to documents, pictures and music*

        Documents   *where letters and other personal documents can be stored*

        Pictures   *access to **Pictures** folder - storage for all types of image file*

continued over

Exercise 11 - Continued

Music	*access to **Music** folder - storage for music and audio files*
Computer	*access to and information about drives and hardware connected to the computer*
Control Panel	*allows customisation of the computer, adding/removal of programs, creation of accounts, etc.*
Devices and Printers	*lets you control various devices such as printers.*
Default Programs	*lets you choose default programs for web browsing, e-mail, playing music, etc.*
Help and Support	*access to Windows help system*

3. Place the cursor over **All Programs**. The installed programs appear here. Some are inside folders such as Games

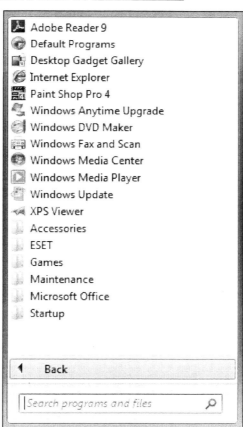

4. Click on the **Games** folder to view the contents.

continued over

Exercise 11 - Continued

Note: *If the **Games** folder only contains **Games Explorer** then the games feature has not been activated. Either turn on the feature (using **Control Panel**, **Programs**, **Programs and Features**, **Turn Windows features on or off**), or move to Step 8 and continue the exercise.*

5. Now click **Solitaire** and you can have a game of cards.

6. This game will allow you to perfect your click and drag technique. The cards are moved by clicking and dragging from one pile to another and turned over by clicking once. They can be placed on one of the four blank areas at the top right by either double clicking or dragging.

Note: *If you don't know how to play **Solitaire**, click on the word **Help** (the menu) at the top of the game then click **View Help**. Scroll down and read the help. Click **Close**, ▭, at the top right of the window to close the **Windows Help and Support** window.*

7. To close **Solitaire**, click on the menu **Game** at the top of the screen and then click **Exit**.

Note: *If you are in the middle of a game you will be given options. Select **Don't save** .*

8. Click the **Start** button, ⊕ then **All Programs**, then **Accessories**. The programs held in the **Accessories** menu are now listed.

9. Press the **Escape** <**Esc**> key on the keyboard to remove the menu. Keep pressing <**Esc**> until no menus are displayed.

10. Click **Start**, place the mouse over **All Programs**, then **Accessories** as before. An easier method to cancel the menus is to click once on the **Desktop**.

11. Click on any blank part of the **Desktop**.

Exercise 12 - Shut Down and Restart the Computer

Guidelines:

It is very important to shut down *Windows* in the correct manner. Temporary files, which are constantly created and stored on the hard disk as *Windows* is working, may cause problems at a later stage if the computer is not shut down properly.

Normally, you should never need to restart the computer while it's switched on. It can, however, be restarted because of problems, without switching off the power. Sometimes a computer locks up, which means that it does not respond to moving the mouse or any key presses. The only course of action in this circumstance is to restart the computer.

Actions:

1. To close *Windows*, locate the **Shut down** button at the bottom of the **Start** menu panel, ⬜Shut down▷. Click the arrow to see more options.

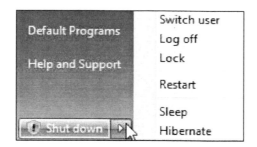

2. Hold the cursor over each of the shut down options to see a description of each option.

Note: *If the keyboard and the mouse are not responding, the computer can usually be* ***Restarted*** *using a* ***Reset*** *button on the front of the computer.*

3. Click the **Shut down** button.

4. Most computers switch their power off as part of the shut down process, but if a message appears informing you to switch off, do so. If the monitor light remains on, switch the monitor off as well.

Note: *Follow these actions every time you wish to turn off the computer. Never switch the power off when the* ***Desktop*** *is displayed. ALWAYS close down Windows properly, using* ***Shut down***.

5. Turn the computer back on.

Exercise 13 - Revision

1. Which part of the computer is used to type information?

2. What is the term for all the parts of a computer, e.g. monitor, mouse, processing unit, etc?

3. What term is used to describe the programs that allow you to use the computer?

4. Why is it important to take a break from looking at the computer screen?

5. What injury can you get when repeating the same movements over a long period of time if your chair and desk are not positioned at the right height?

6. When might you have to use a **password**?

7. What are **icons**?

8. What does this mouse pointer mean: ?

9. How do you display the **Start** menu?

10. Which option do you select from the **Start** menu to close the computer down?

Note: Check the **Answers** section at the end of the guide.

Section 2

Windows

By the end of this Section you should be able to:

Recognise Windows

Understand how Windows Work

Open and Close Windows

Maximise, Minimise and Restore Windows

Resize and Move Windows

Use Scroll Bars

Understand Dialog Boxes

Change Basic Settings

Exercise 14 - About Windows

Guidelines:

Windows gets its name from the fact that everything you do on the computer is shown in a window. Think of working with the computer as looking through a window to see the information stored inside the computer. Below is a document open in a word processing program which is running in a window.

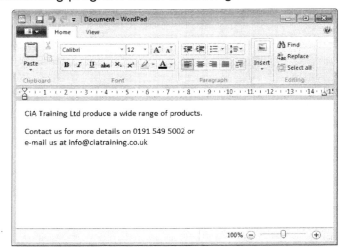

Windows come in various sizes, but are always rectangular or square and have several features in common (described in the next exercise). Many windows can be open at the same time and are often placed on top of one another. The **Taskbar** will show you the windows that are open. Look at the diagram below:

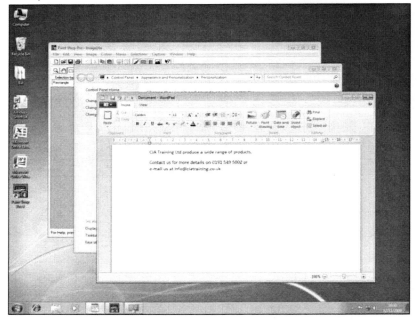

There are three windows open on the **Desktop**, one on top of another. The following exercises will show you how to work with windows, although you have already encountered this by working through earlier exercises.

Exercise 15 - Opening Windows

Guidelines:

As explained earlier, windows are rectangular areas of the screen in which programs are run, contents of disks are shown, etc. Many windows can be open at a time, each with a different task being performed.

Actions:

1. Click the **Start** button, 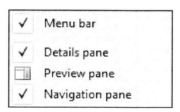, on the **Taskbar** and select **Computer** from the right part of the **Start** menu. The **Computer** window will open (some icons may be different to those shown below).

2. Notice that the open window is represented by a button on the **Taskbar**, e.g. or .

3. Click the **Organize** button on the **Toolbar** to display a list of options. Notice that some of the items are ghosted, greyed out; this means that they are not available in the present circumstances.

4. Move the cursor over **Layout** to display a list of the parts of this window that will be displayed. If there is a tick next to the part, this means it will be displayed in the window. If **Menu Bar** does not have a tick, click on it now so that it will be shown.

✓	Menu bar
✓	Details pane
☐	Preview pane
✓	Navigation pane

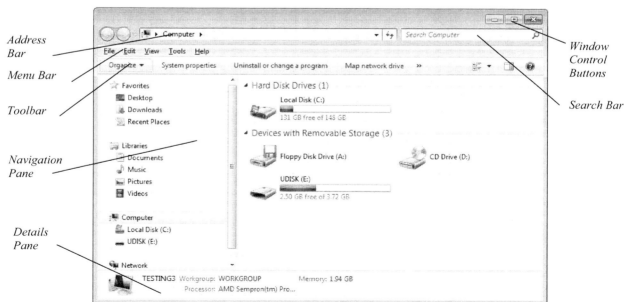

Address Bar, *Menu Bar*, *Toolbar*, *Navigation Pane*, *Details Pane*, *Window Control Buttons*, *Search Bar*

continued over

Exercise 15 - Continued

5. Each window is similar in its construction. At the top right of all window are three **Window Control Buttons**. These are the **Minimize,** [icon], **Maximize,** [icon] and **Close,** [icon], buttons. Some windows have **Back** and **Forward** buttons at the top left, an **Address bar** to show where you are looking, and then a **Search bar** to allow you to search within the current window. Some windows have a **Title bar** across the top.

Note: *If the window fills the screen the centre button will be* ***Restore Down,*** *[icon], click this button to reduce the size of the window.*

6. Below the **Address bar** is the **Menu bar** (for most windows). Click the **Tools** menu, then click **Folder options** from the menu to view a dialog box showing the available options.

7. Click the **Cancel** button in the dialog box to close it.

8. Below the **Menu bar** is the **Toolbar** (some windows may have more than one). Click the drop down arrow on the **Views** button, [icon]. Make sure **Tiles** view is selected, either by dragging the slider or clicking on the **Tiles** option.

Note: *The appearance of the* ***View*** *button changes depending on which view is currently selected. Views are covered in a later exercise.*

9. Click on any blank part of the window to close the menu.

10. Click the **Organize** button, move the cursor over **Layout** and click **Menu bar** again to remove it.

11. Within the window, point to and click the **Hard Disk Drive** icon,  - it changes to [icon] when selected.

Note: *The* ***Hard Disk Drive*** *is where all the information is stored on a computer. It is nearly always known as the* ***C*** *drive, written as* ***[C:]*** *or* ***Local Disk (C:)***.

12. Right click on the icon for the **Hard Disk Drive** and select **Properties**. This dialog box contains information about the drive including the amount of used and free space.

13. Click **Cancel** to close the dialog box. Leave the **Computer** window open.

Exercise 16 - Closing Windows

Guidelines:

The **Close** button, ▣, at the top right of every window, closes it and any task being performed within it.

Actions:

1. In the **Computer** window, click the [System properties] button.

2. Look at the **Address bar**. You are looking inside the **System** folder which is found within the **Control Panel**.

3. Click the **Back** button, ⬅, in the top left of the window to close this display and go back to the main **Computer** display.

4. Click the **Close** button, ▣, of the **Computer** window.

Close Button

5. The window is closed and **Computer** icon on the **Taskbar** becomes inactive. The icon is not removed from the **Taskbar** if it has been 'pinned' to it (placed permanently there).

6. Click the **Start** button, then **All Programs**, then **Accessories**.

7. Click **Calculator** to start it. A window opens and an icon appears on the **Taskbar**.

8. Hold down the <**Alt**> key on the keyboard and press the <**F4**> key. This is another way to close a window. When the window closes, the icon disappears from the **Taskbar**.

Exercise 17 - Resizing and Moving Windows

Guidelines

Windows can be made to fill the screen (**maximised**), or to be hidden completely (**minimised**). **Restoring** a window changes a maximised window back to its previous intermediate size. In this format, the size and position of the window can be changed.

Actions:

1. Click the **Start** button and select **Computer**. If the **Restore Down** button, , is displayed near the top right corner of the window, click it now.

2. Click the **Maximize** button, , of the **Computer** window. The window will now fill the screen.

3. When a window is maximised, the **Maximize** button is replaced by the **Restore Down** button, . Click the **Restore Down** button to change the maximised window back to its previous size.

4. The **Minimize** button, , hides the window completely. Click the **Minimize** button of the **Computer** window.

5. However, the program in the window is not closed and the window can be re-activated by clicking on its button on the **Taskbar**. Click the **Computer** button, or , on the **Taskbar**.

6. Make sure the **Computer** window is not maximised and move the mouse pointer over the blue area at the top of the window.

7. Click the mouse button, hold it down and drag the pointer down the screen. The entire window will move down, be careful not to hide any part of the window.

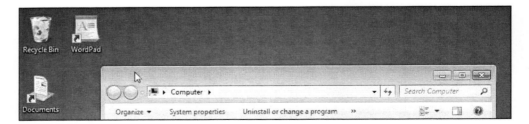

8. Release the mouse button.

continued over

Exercise 17 - Continued

9. The size of the window can also be changed. Move the mouse pointer over the right edge of the window, until the pointer changes to a double headed arrow, 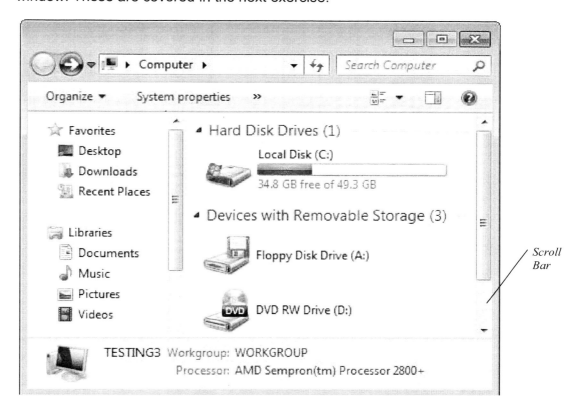.

10. Click and drag to the right, and then release the mouse button, to increase the width of the window.

11. Placing the mouse over a corner of a window allows a two-direction change in the size of a window. Place the mouse pointer over the bottom right corner of the **Computer** window.

12. The cursor changes to two headed diagonal arrow, Click and drag a small amount in any direction to change the size and scale of the window.

13. Click and drag the bottom right corner of the **Computer** window in towards the centre of the window to make it smaller. When the window is too small to display all the information it contains, scroll bars will be added to the window. These are covered in the next exercise.

Scroll
Bar

14. Click and drag the bottom right corner of the **Computer** window outwards to make it larger. Enlarge the window until no scroll bars are seen.

15. Close the **Computer** window using the **Close** button, .

Exercise 18 - Scroll Bars

Guidelines:

When a window in any program is too small to display all the information in it, then the window automatically adds **Scroll Bars**. Scroll Bars are added horizontally and/or vertically, depending on the hidden information.

Actions:

1. Click **Start**, then click **Control Panel** from the right side of the **Start** menu. Make sure the **Control Panel** window is not maximised, click **Restore Down**, ⬜, if necessary.

2. Click **Category** on the right of the window to display a list of options.

3. Select **Large icons** from the list. There are now too many icons to display inside this window.

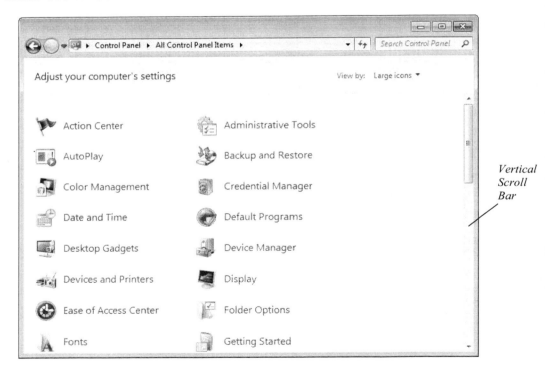

Vertical Scroll Bar

4. The window now has a vertical scroll bar, which can be used to scroll down the window in order to see all of the available information. A scroll bar consists of scroll arrows, top and bottom, a scroll button (proportional to the window) and a grey bar to move the button into (the bar represents the extent of the window).

continued over

Exercise 18 - Continued

5. Click on the down arrow of the right vertical scroll bar to move the viewed area down the window by a small amount. Continue to do this until the scroll button is at the bottom of the scroll bar.

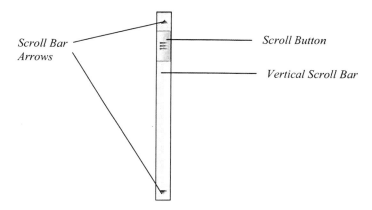

Scroll Bar Arrows

Scroll Button

Vertical Scroll Bar

Note: *To move the viewed area of a window by a block at a time, click once on the vertical scroll bar between the scroll button and the top or bottom arrow.*

6. When the **Scroll Button** is at the bottom of the **Scroll Bar**, click and drag the button back up to the top. This is another method of scrolling.

Note: *The size of the scroll button compared to the size of the bar represents how much of the whole window content is currently being displayed.*

7. Click **Large icons** on the right of the window and select **Category** to return to the original display format.

8. Leave the **Control Panel** window open.

Exercise 19 - Dialog Boxes

Guidelines:

The usual way of changing any settings or choosing options in a *Windows* application is by using dialog boxes. A dialog box is a small window that contains various options, choices and commands. There are many different ways of choosing options in a dialog box, such as buttons which are clicked on, boxes which have crosses inserted in them, buttons which make lists of options appear, etc.

Some of these different ways of choosing options are:

Tabs

These are small tabs at the top of the dialog box which, when clicked on, change the contents of the dialog box to a different set of choices on a different 'page'.

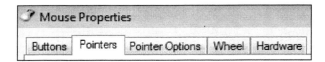

Drop Down Lists

To make a selection, click on the arrow button at the right of the box and a list of options appears. If the list is very long, there will be a scroll bar at the right. Scroll down the list if necessary to find the required option and click on it. The list disappears and the selection appears in the box.

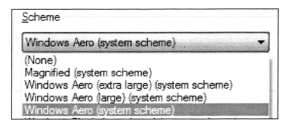

Some short lists are permanently displayed and it is only necessary to click the required option to select it. These are called **List boxes**.

Option Buttons

Two or more option buttons may be displayed and a choice made from the selection. Only one option from the available selection can be chosen at a time. The selected option has a small black circle in the white button.

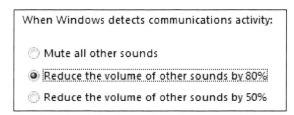

continued over

Exercise 19 - Continued

Check Boxes

These show options which can be turned on or off. To change the status of a check box, click on it. A ✔ (tick) appears in the box if the option is selected. Any number of check boxes can be selected at any time.

Number Selection

When a number is required, it can be either typed into the box or the up and down 'spinners' can be used to increase or decrease the number.

Spinner

Text Boxes

Any text can be entered in this box. These boxes are sometimes combined with list boxes, in which case the text can be either entered or selected. These are called **Combo** boxes.

Slider Controls

Sliders are used to select a setting from an available range. Use the mouse to click and drag the slider until it is over the required setting.

Actions:

1. The **Control Panel** should still be open. This contains many tools used for configuring and changing the way *Windows* looks and acts.

2. In the **Control Panel** window, click on the **Appearance and Personalization** option, then on **Personalization**.

3. Click on the text **Change mouse pointers** on the left. The **Mouse Properties** dialog box now appears.

4. Use the tabs at the top of the dialog box to see examples of many of the different types of controls. Do not change any settings.

5. Click the **Cancel** button to close the dialog box without making any changes. Click the **Back** button until the original **Control Panel** window is displayed then leave it open.

Exercise 20 - Changing Basic Settings

Guidelines:

The computer has a built in clock and calendar. On occasion, the time or date may need to be changed. Modern computers can be set to adjust automatically for the clocks going forward or back. Take care if planning to alter the date or time on a networked computer, as the system may need to have all components synchronised. Sounds can be assigned to various events in *Windows* by using the **Sounds** dialog box. A list of events is shown; those with sounds attached are indicated by a speaker icon.

Actions:

1. From the **Control Panel**, select the **Clock, Language and Region** option, then **Date and Time**. The **Date and Time** dialog box is displayed.

2. Check that the date and time are correct. If not, click **Change date and time**. Make the necessary changes using the appropriate boxes and then click **OK**.

3. Check the **Time Zone** area and make sure that the computer is using the correct time zone. If not, click **Change time zone**. Make the necessary change using the drop down list and then click **OK**.

4. Click **Cancel** to close the dialog box without keeping any of the changes or click **OK** to accept the changes.

5. To display the **Date and Time** using an alternative method, click on the **Time** on the right of the **Taskbar**.

6. Click on a blank part of the **Desktop** to close the date and time settings.

continued over

Exercise 20 - Continued

7.   Use the **Back** button to return to the original **Control Panel** window. Click **Hardware and Sound**, then click **Sound**. Click the **Sounds** tab.

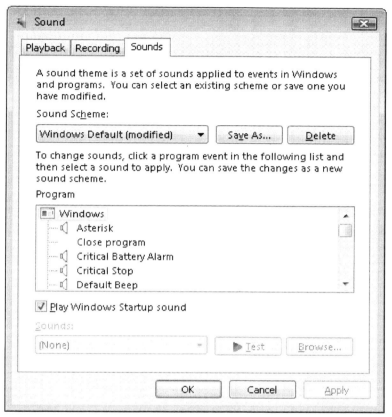

8.   Select any of the **Program Events** with a sound attached, (🔊), and click the **Test** button, [▶ _Test_], to hear the sound.

Note: The speakers need to be attached, switched on and the volume controls set.

9.   Click **Cancel** to close the dialog box.

10.   Click on the volume control icon 🔊, on the right of the **Taskbar**, to display a simplified **Volume** slider.

11.   Click and drag the slider to vary the sound level then click on a blank area of **Desktop** to remove it.

*Note: To change the volume for speakers and applications, click **Mixer** on the slider.*

12.   Use the **Close** button, 🗙, to close the **Control Panel** window.

Exercise 21 - Revision

1. What appears on the **Taskbar** when a window is open?

2. Open your named folder window using the **Start** menu.

3. Minimise the window.

4. View the window again and maximise it.

5. Use the **Restore Down** button to reduce the size of the window so that it does not fill the screen.

6. If there are no scroll bars showing, click and drag the bottom edge of the window up to make it smaller until the scroll bars appear.

7. Return the window to its original size.

8. Close the window.

Note: Check the **Answers** section at the end of the guide.

Section 3

File Management

By the end of this Section you should be able to:

Understand the Structure of Files and Folders on a Computer

Create Folders

Move and Copy Files and Folders

Select Multiple Files

Rename Files and Folders

Delete Files and Folders

Use the Recycle Bin

Print File Structure

Exercise 22 - Understanding Files and Folders

Guidelines:

In order to assist in storing and finding files and programs on the hard disk, *Windows* uses **Folders**. The hard disk, CD and floppy disk are split into many folders, each containing files related to a specific task or purpose. You can create and delete your own folders, and move files around from folder to folder. A folder may also contain other folders, dividing the disk even further. The concept is like organising a filing cabinet by having separate drawers and files for each particular task.

A folder in *Windows* appears as an icon, with the name of the folder printed next to or underneath it. When the icon is double clicked, the folder opens, and its contents appear in a new window.

The **Documents** window and the **Computer** window allow you to view and organise files and folders. The program behind these windows is called **Windows Explorer**. It can be used to control the copying, moving, creating and deleting of files and folders, known as **File Management**.

Folders can be grouped into **Libraries**. **Libraries** are just collections of folders; they do not exist as folders themselves. The library examined in this guide is the **Documents** library.

Actions:

1. Click **Documents** in the **Start Menu**. This will run **Windows Explorer** and display the contents of the **Documents** library.

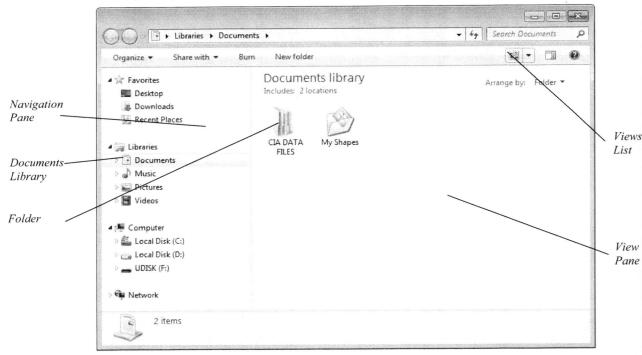

continued over

Exercise 22 - Continued

Note: *The contents of your **Documents** library may be different to that above. There are also different views of the same information.*

2.   Click the drop down arrow on the **Views** button, 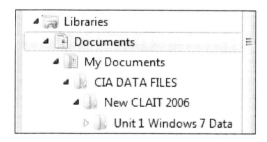 and make sure the slider is positioned next to **Tiles**. Views are covered in the next exercise.

3.   One way to navigate through the folders on your computer is to use the **Navigation pane** on the left. Move the cursor to this area and notice that the **Documents** library has an ▷ icon in front of it. This means that the folder has subfolders.

4.   Click once on ▷, the subfolders are displayed underneath the main folder and the icon changes to a ◢ icon. This is called **expanding** a folder.

5.   To hide the subfolders, click the ◢ icon next to **Documents**. The ◢ icon changes to a ▷ icon again and the subfolders or files are hidden. This is called **collapsing** a folder.

6.   Make sure the **Documents** library is expanded in the **Navigation pane**.

7.   Expand **My Documents** folder, then the **CIA DATA FILES** folder, then **New CLAIT 2006**.

Note: *If the supplied data files were installed in a different folder, they should be located by navigating through the folder structure.*

8.   Click once on the **Unit 1 Windows 7 Data** folder. The contents of this folder will be displayed on the right, in the **View pane**.

9.   There is another way of navigating. Click the **Documents** library in the **Navigation pane** to return to the original view.

10. In the **View pane**, double click **CIA DATA FILES** to display its contents.

11. In the **View pane**, double click **New CLAIT 2006**, then **Unit 1 Windows 7 Data**. The contents of this folder will be displayed again in the **View pane**.

12. Leave the **Documents** window open.

Exercise 23 - Views

Guidelines:

The contents of folders can be displayed in a number of different views.

Actions:

1. The contents of the **Unit 1 Windows 7 Data** should be displayed. Click the **Views** button drop down arrow, and select **Medium Icons**.

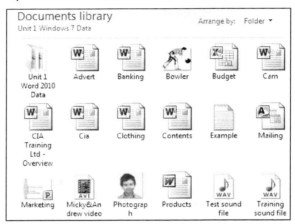

2. Notice that each type of file has a different type of icon to represent it. The icons for some files such as image files and presentations, even give an indication of the file content.

3. Click the **Views** drop down button again and select **Details**. The folder contents are now listed with properties like **Date modified**, **Type** and **Size** displayed.

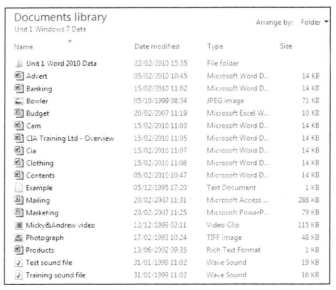

4. Try different views then leave the display open in **Details** view.

Exercise 24 - Creating a New Folder

Guidelines:

A well-structured storage system makes it easy to locate the required files quickly. From time to time you will need to create new folders in which to store your files. Whenever a library or folder contents is displayed in *Windows Explorer*, a new folder can be created by using the **New folder** button. A new folder is created and its icon displayed. Enter the name of the new folder, then click once anywhere away from the folder.

Alternatively, clicking once with the **right** mouse button in the **View pane** will display a shortcut menu. Select **New** and then **Folder** to create a new folder.

Actions:

1.   The contents of the **Unit 1 Windows 7 Data** should be displayed in **Details view**.

2.   Click **New folder** on the toolbar. A new folder is created and the name is highlighted in blue.

Name		Date modified	Type
New folder		18/11/2009 19:43	File folder
Unit 1 Word 2007 Data		18/11/2009 15:26	File folder

3.   Enter the name **Test** and then press <**Enter**>.

4.   The folder named **Test** is now created within the **Unit 1 Windows 7 Data** folder and immediately appears in the **Folder** pane list. Display the contents of the **Test** folder by clicking it in the **Navigation pane**. It is empty.

5.   Close the **Test** folder using the **Back** button, ⬅, on the toolbar.

6.   Click the **Forward** button, ➡, to open the **Test** folder.

7.   Right click in a blank part of the **View pane**, move the cursor over **New** in the shortcut menu, and select **Folder** from the second shortcut menu. A new folder is created within the **Test** folder.

8.   Enter your first name as the title for this folder, press <**Enter**>.

9.   Click the chevrons, « , on the **Address Bar**, next to the folder icon and select ☐ Documents from the drop down list, to return to the **Documents** folder.

10.   Leave **Documents** open for the next exercise.

Exercise 25 - Moving Files and Folders

Guidelines:

A file or folder can be moved from one location to another from within a single window. The result of the operation depends on the location of the source and destination. Dragging an item from one location to another on the same drive defaults to a MOVE operation, dragging from one drive to another, results in a COPY operation.

When dragging, ensure that the destination for the file is visible in the **Navigation pane** (expand a folder if necessary) at the left, and that the correct destination is highlighted in blue.

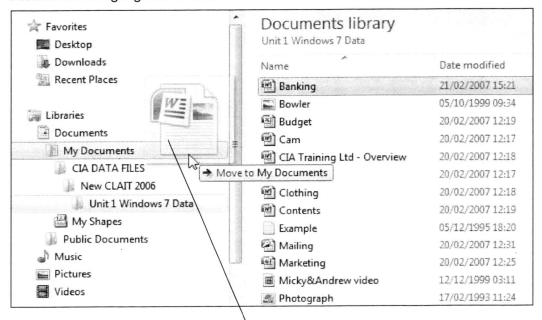

Banking *file being moved from* ***Unit 1 Windows 7 Data*** *folder to* ***My Documents*** *(in this example)*

A message box may appear showing the file flying from one location to another. Alternatively, clicking and dragging a file icon with the **right** mouse button will produce a shortcut menu when the button is released.

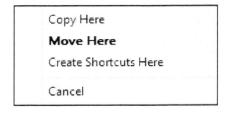

The file can then be either moved or copied to the destination.

continued over

Exercise 25 - Continued

Actions:

1. In the **Navigation** pane of the **Documents** window, expand the libraries and folders until **Unit 1 Windows 7 Data** is displayed.

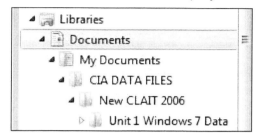

2. Click **Unit 1 Windows 7 Data** to display its contents in the **View pane**.

3. Double click the **Test** folder in the **View pane** to display its contents.

4. Click and drag the **yourname** folder from the **Test** folder on the right to the **My Documents** folder in the **Navigation pane**. Release the mouse button. This is a move operation, notice how the **yourname** folder disappears from the **Test** folder and now appears under **My Documents**.

5. Click on the **Unit 1 Windows 7 Data** folder to display the files in the folder.

6. Click and drag the **Cia** file to the **Test** folder within the **Unit 1 Windows 7 Data** folder. Release the mouse button.

7. Now move the file **Example** (from the **Unit 1 Windows 7 Data** folder) to the **Test** folder.

8. View the contents of the **Test** folder by clicking on its folder icon in the **Navigation pane**. The two recently moved files should be there.

9. View the contents of the **Unit 1 Windows 7 Data** folder. The files **Cia** and **Example** should no longer be listed. They have been moved.

Exercise 26 - Copying Files and Folders

Guidelines:

Files and folders can be copied in various ways, depending on where they are being copied to. When copying a file or folder between locations on the <u>same</u> drive, you must hold down the **<Ctrl>** key when dragging the file over its destination. A **Tooltip** appears next to the mouse pointer as you drag the file, indicating that it is being *copied*.

When copying a file <u>from one drive to another</u>, e.g. backing up from **C:** to the floppy drive **A:**, you only need to drag the file to its destination drive and it will be copied. To be sure of copying rather than moving a file, some people prefer to click and drag a file icon with the <u>right</u> mouse button. This displays a shortcut menu when the button is released, from which **Copy Here** can be selected.

Actions:

1. Display the contents of the **Test** folder. It should contain the two files, **Cia** and **Example** moved there in the last exercise.

2. To copy a file, click once on the **Cia** file and hold down the **<Ctrl>** key.

3. Drag the file over to **Unit 1 Windows 7 Data**, (notice the **Screen Tip**).

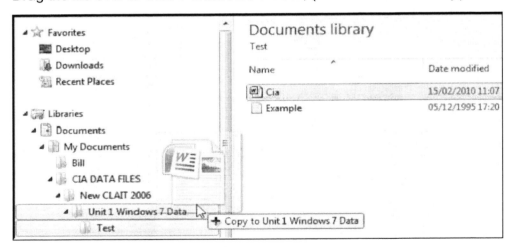

4. Release the mouse button, then the **<Ctrl>** key, when over the folder. The file remains in the **Test** folder but a copy will now exist in **Unit 1 Windows 7 Data**.

5. To copy the **Test** folder, click on the **Unit 1 Windows 7 Data** icon in the **Navigation** pane to display its contents in the **View** pane.

6. Click on the **Test** folder, hold down **<Ctrl>** and drag the folder to **Unit 1 Windows 7 Data**. Release the mouse button then **<Ctrl>**. The folder is copied and the name changes to **Test - Copy** (duplicate names are not allowed in the same folder). Look in the **Unit 1 Windows 7 Data** folder. The **Test - Copy** folder icon appears.

continued over

Exercise 26 - Continued

Note: *If this folder had been copied to any other location, where there was not an existing folder with the name Test, the name of the copied item would remain as* ***Test****.*

7.　Using the **right** mouse button, click and drag the **Example** file icon from the **Test** folder (within **Unit 1 Windows 7 Data**) back to the **Unit 1 Windows 7 Data** folder. Release the mouse button.

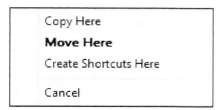

8.　Select **Copy Here** from the shortcut menu.

Note: *Click and drag with the **right** mouse button is the 'safe' option because it always gives a choice of **move** or **copy** regardless of the location and its destination.*

9.　The files **Cia** and **Example** should both still be listed in the **Test** folder. Open the **Unit 1 Windows 7 Data** folder and confirm that both files are also listed there.

10.　Leave the **Unit 1 Windows 7 Data** folder open for the next exercise.

Note: ***Cut****, **Copy** and **Paste** can also be used to copy and move files and folders using the **Organize** button,* | Organize ▾ | *drop down or the quick key presses* *<**Ctrl X**>, <**Ctrl C**> and <**Ctrl V**>.*

Exercise 27 - Selecting Multiple Files

Guidelines:

Often in file management, more than one file at a time needs to be copied, moved or deleted. This means that multiple files need to be selected. Use the following methods to select multiple files:

Actions:

1. View the contents of the **Unit 1 Windows 7 Data** folder as a list, by clicking the drop down arrow on the **View** button,  and selecting **List**.

*Note: Remember, the appearance of the **View** button changes with the currently selected view.*

2. Before selecting files, there is another viewing option which may be useful. Click the **Organize** button and select **Folder and search options**.

3. In the **Folder Options** dialog box, select the **View** tab.

4. Look for the following line in the **Advanced settings** list:

5. Click the line to remove the tick (the option is de-selected) and file extensions will now be displayed. Click **OK**.

Note: File extensions are short codes such as .docx that are displayed after file names to indicate the exact file type. They can provide useful information but they do not affect the operation of file management techniques in any way.

6. To select a range of files, click once on the first of the files required, **Banking.docx**, hold down the <**Shift**> key on the keyboard, then click on the last file of the required range, **Clothing.docx**. Release the <**Shift**> key. All the files in between will be selected.

continued over

Exercise 27 - Continued

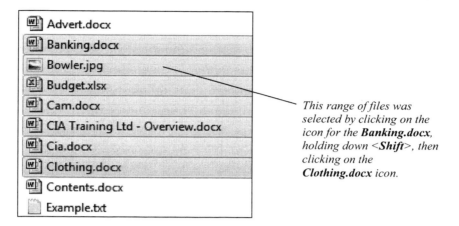

*This range of files was selected by clicking on the icon for the **Banking.docx**, holding down <Shift>, then clicking on the **Clothing.docx** icon.*

7.   Click away from the selection to cancel it.

8.   To select multiple files that are not in a range, hold down <**Ctrl**> on the keyboard and click on all the files to be selected, as below.

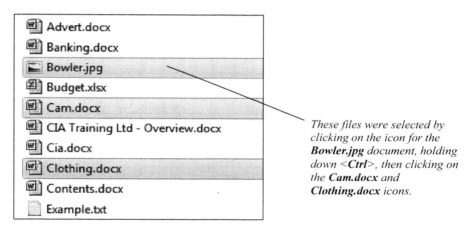

*These files were selected by clicking on the icon for the **Bowler.jpg** document, holding down <**Ctrl**>, then clicking on the **Cam.docx** and **Clothing.docx** icons.*

9.   Click away from the selection to cancel it.

10.   To select all the files and folders in the **View** window, either click **Organize** and choose **Select all** or press <**Ctrl A**> on the keyboard.

11.   Click away from the selection.

Note: *Once multiple files have been selected, dragging and dropping any one of the selected files will move or copy all the files in the selection. Multiple files can also be selected for deletion.*

12.   Leave the window open.

Exercise 28 - Renaming Files and Folders

Guidelines:

Files and folders can be renamed at any time to help with their management.

Actions:

1. After creating a copy of the folder **Test** in Exercise 26, there are now two folders with similar names. The **Test - Copy** folder within **Unit 1 Windows 7 Data** is to be renamed to avoid confusion. In the **View** pane, right click on the **Test - Copy** folder. A shortcut menu will appear, similar to that below.

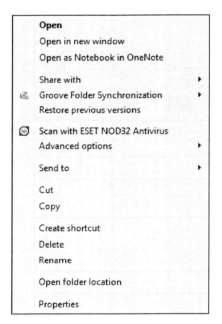

2. Select the **Rename** option from the shortcut menu.

3. The **Test - Copy** name is highlighted. Type in **Exercises**. Press **<Enter>**.

Note: If you click on a file or folder, wait, and click again it is possible to rename it. This happens accidentally sometimes when a double click is performed too slowly.

4. Renaming files is performed in the same way. Display the contents of the **Exercises** folder. Right click on the **Example** file and select **Rename** from the shortcut menu.

5. Type in **Text File** as the new name and press **<Enter>**.

6. Leave the **Exercises** contents displayed for the next exercise.

Exercise 29 - Deleting Files and Folders

Guidelines:

Files and folders can be deleted in three main ways:

- Select the icon by clicking it, then press the <**Delete**> key.

- Click once on the file / folder with the **right** mouse button then select **Delete**.

- Drag the file / folder over the **Recycle Bin** icon on the **Desktop** then release the icon "into" the bin (the **Recycle Bin** is covered in the next exercise).

Note: *The result of deleting files depends on where the files are located. If the file is on a hard disk, then the file is removed (after a confirmation prompt), and placed in the **Recycle Bin**. If the file is on removable media such as a memory stick, a message appears checking if the user is sure that the file is to be deleted, as it will be deleted permanently.*

Actions:

1. In the **Exercises** window, click on the **Text File** icon to select it, if not already selected. Press the <**Delete**> key. A message appears, confirming that the file is to be removed.

2. Clicking **Yes** would move the file to the **Recycle Bin**, but for now select **No**.

3. Click once on the **Text File** icon with the right mouse button, then select **Delete** from the shortcut menu. At the message, select **No** to keep the file.

4. Click and drag the **Text File** icon over the **Recycle Bin** icon on the **Desktop** and release the mouse button (reduce the size of the window if necessary to see the **Recycle Bin** icon).

5. The icon disappears from the **Exercises** window and the file is moved to the **Recycle Bin**. Delete the **Test** folder from **Unit 1 Windows 7 Data** and **Your name** folder from **My Documents**, using any of the above methods.

Note: *When a folder is deleted, a **Delete Folder** message is displayed, click **Yes** to move the folder and all its contents to the **Recycle Bin**.*

Exercise 30 - The Recycle Bin

Guidelines:

When files or folders are deleted, they are not instantly removed from the hard disk. They are held in the **Recycle Bin**, whose icon can be seen on the **Desktop**. The **Recycle Bin Desktop** icon changes according to whether it contains any files, 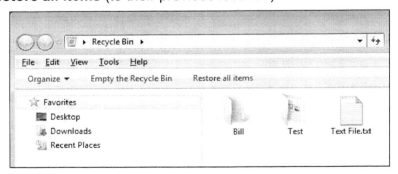, or is empty, . All deleted items are stored there until the **Recycle Bin** is emptied. Until then, the files can be restored to their original location.

Once the **Recycle Bin** is emptied the contents are **permanently** deleted and **can no longer be recovered**. Deleting individual items from the **Recycle Bin** also permanently removes them.

Note: *Files or folders deleted from removable media are **not** held in the **Recycle Bin**, but are deleted instantly.*

Actions:

1.   Double click the **Recycle Bin** icon on the **Desktop** to display its contents, a list of all items that have been deleted.

Note: *The content of the **Recycle Bin** is dependent on when it was last emptied. **Text File.txt**, the **Test** folder and **your name** folder will be in the **Recycle Bin**. However, you may need to scroll to see them.*

2.   When the **Recycle Bin** is selected, the buttons on the toolbar change to include **Empty the Recycle Bin** (permanently delete all the listed items) and **Restore all items** (to their previous location).

3.   To restore a file or a folder, select it from the list, the **Restore all items** text will change to **Restore this item**. Click **Text File.txt** and click **Restore this item**, the file is removed from the **Recycle Bin** and placed where it was before deletion (missing folders will be recreated where necessary).

4.   Close the **Recycle Bin** window.

5.   Click with the right mouse button on the **Recycle Bin** icon on the **Desktop**. From the shortcut menu, select **Empty Recycle Bin**. A message appears to confirm the action. Select **Yes** if you are happy to remove all items, if not, select **No**.

Exercise 31 - Printing File Structure

Guidelines:

As part of the assessment for this unit, you may be required to make a printout of the file structure. This is to demonstrate that you have been able to move and copy files and folders, create new folders and so on. Before starting this exercise, make sure the printer is correctly loaded with paper.

Actions:

1. Select the **Unit 1 Windows 7 Data** folder in the **Navigation pane** so that its contents are displayed. Select **Details** view for the contents.

2. To make a copy of what you can see on the screen (this is called a screen dump), press the **Print Screen** key at the top right of the keyboard.

Note: The image is copied to the Windows **Clipboard**, which will be discussed later.

3. Now you need to start a program that allows you to paste in the image and print it out. You are going to use *Word*. Select **Start | All Programs | Microsoft Office | Microsoft Office Word 2007**.

4. *Word* starts. To paste in the image, click the **Paste** button, in the **Clipboard** group on the **Home** tab. The page now shows the screen dump.

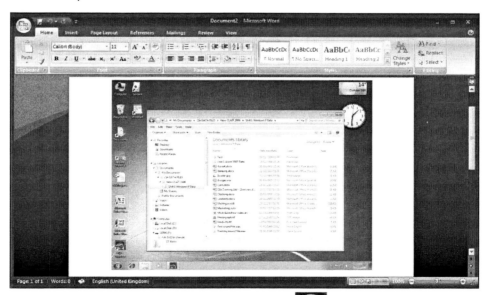

5. To obtain a printout, click the **Office Button**, and click **Print** and click **OK** in the dialog box.

6. Close *Word* by clicking the **Office Button** again and selecting **Exit Word** from the menus. Do not save when prompted.

7. Close the **Documents** window.

Exercise 32 - Revision

1. Open the **Computer** window.

2. In the **Navigation** pane, expand **Computer**.

3. Display the contents of the **C:** drive in the **View** pane.

4. Change the view to **Medium icons**, then to **Details**.

5. Close the **Computer** window and open **Documents**.

6. Expand libraries and folders until **Unit 1 Windows 7 Data** folder is shown.

7. Display the contents of the **Unit 1 Windows 7 Data** folder. How many yellow folders does it contain?

8. Collapse the folder where the files are stored.

9. Close the window.

Note: Check the **Answers** section at the end of the guide.

1 yellow folder-

Exercise 33 - Revision

1. Open the **Documents** window.

2. Create a new folder within **My Documents**.

3. Name it **Structure**.

4. Copy the following files from the **Unit 1 Windows 7 Data** folder to the new folder (**Structure**): **Banking, Mickey&Andrew video, Marketing**, and **Test sound file**.

5. Create another new folder within **Structure** and name it **Media**.

6. Move **Mickey&Andrew video** and **Test sound file** from **Structure** to the **Media** folder.

7. Print the file structure, with the **Documents** and **Structure** folders expanded and the contents of **Structure** being displayed in **Details** view.

8. Copy the **Banking** file from **Structure** to the **Media** folder.

9. Rename the **Banking** file as **Money** in the **Media** folder.

10. Print the file structure again, displaying the contents of the **Media** folder.

11. Delete the **Structure** and **Exercises** folders and all their contents.

12. Close the window.

*Note: Check the **Answers** section at the end of the guide.*

Section 4

Introduction to Word Processing

By the end of this Section you should be able to:

Appreciate the Advantages of Word Processed Documents
Start Microsoft *Word*
Recognise the Screen Layout
Exit Microsoft *Word*

Exercise 34 - Starting Word

Guidelines:

Although simple text editors, e.g. *NotePad* supplied with *Windows*, allow you to create documents, a word processor such as *Word* provides much more control over how they look. It is possible to format text - to make it more attractive and well presented. A word processor shows exactly how a document will look when it is printed. This is known as **WYSIWYG**: **W**hat **Y**ou **S**ee **I**s **W**hat **Y**ou **G**et.

There are numerous ways to start *Word*, but the following method is recommended for beginners.

Actions:

1. When the computer is started, the *Windows* **Desktop** is automatically shown. Click once on to show the **Start menu**.

2. Click **All Programs**, then click on the **Microsoft Office** entry and then on Microsoft Office Word 2007.

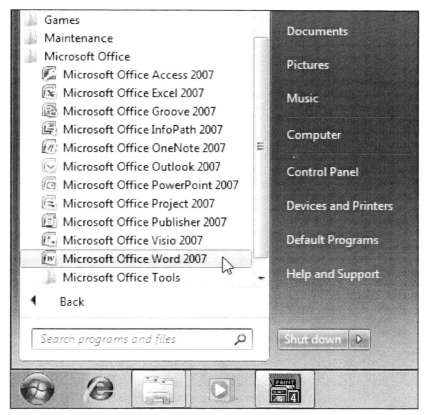

Note: The listing under **All Programs** and the list at the left of the **Start** menu will be different depending on the software currently installed on the PC.

Exercise 35 - The Layout of the Word Screen

Guidelines:

In previous versions of *Microsoft Office* applications, commands were controlled by a series of menus and toolbars. *Word 2007* has replaced these with a **Ribbon** which is displayed at the top of the application window. The **Ribbon** contains buttons and drop down lists to control the operation of *Word*. The **Ribbon** is divided into a series of **Tabs**, each one of which has a set of controls specific to a certain function or process. On each tab, the controls are further divided into separate **Groups** of connected functions.

Some tabs can be selected manually, some only appear when certain operations are active, for example only when a picture is active, will **Picture Tools** tabs be displayed on the **Ribbon**.

Above the **Ribbon** is the **Quick Access Toolbar** which contains a few popular command buttons. By default this toolbar has three buttons, **Save**, **Undo** and **Repeat**. This toolbar can be customised by adding further buttons. When *Word* starts, the following screen appears:

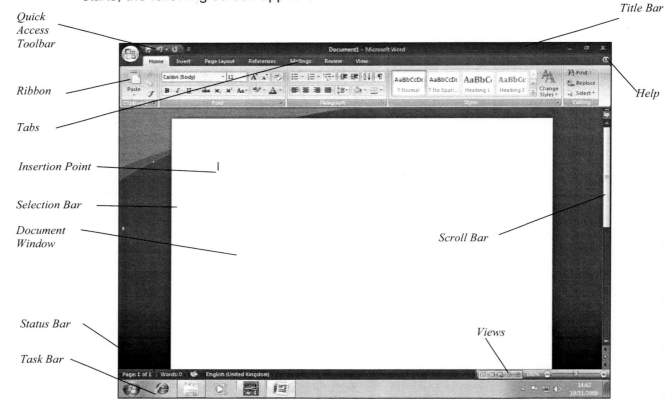

Actions:

1.	Look at the top line, the **Title Bar**, displaying **Microsoft Word**. It also shows the title of the current document.

continued over

Exercise 35 - Continued

2.   Below that is the **Ribbon**, where commands are chosen using the mouse. It is made up of **Tabs** (the words at the top of the ribbon, which illuminate when the mouse is rolled over them), **Groups** (the boxes which spread horizontally across the ribbon, distinguishable by their names at the bottom of each) and **Commands** (the icons within groups which perform different actions).

3.   Find the bar at the bottom of the screen. This is called the **Status Bar**, where the page number will be displayed.

4.   The main part of the screen shows a blank document. The default view, shown here is **Print Layout** view.

5.   In the top left corner of the screen, click the **Office Button**, ![office button] , and select **New**. This dialog box deals with opening and creating a new document.

6.   Click ![close] to close the **New Document** dialog box.

7.   On the **Ribbon**, the **Home** tab should be selected. Other basic tabs are available.

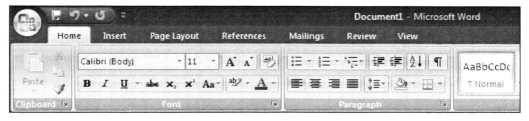

*Part of the **Ribbon** displaying the **Home** tab*

Note: *Any buttons displayed in pale grey are called ghosted and are not available to be selected at present.*

8.   Notice how the buttons on the **Ribbon** are divided into **Groups** (**Clipboard**, **Font**, **Paragraph**, etc.).

Note: *The display of buttons on the **Ribbon** is dynamic. That is it will change according to how much space there is available. If the window is not maximised or the screen resolution is anything other than 1024 by 768, the **Ribbon** will not always appear as shown in this guide.*

9.   Place the cursor over one of the buttons. A **ToolTip** appears which give more information and an alternative key press for the function if available.

10.   Some buttons produce immediate effects, like the **Bold**, **Italic** and **Underline** buttons in the **Font** group.

continued over

Exercise 35 - Continued

11. Buttons with a drop down arrow lead to further options. Click the **Select** button, which is found in the **Editing** group. A list of further options is displayed. Click on the white page area to close the menu.

12. Some options will display a dialog box which needs data to be entered. Click the **Replace** button, the **Replace** dialog box is displayed. Click the **Cancel** button in the dialog box to remove it.

13. Some groups have a dialog box launcher to the right of the group name, e.g. the **Font** group, [Font].

14. Click the **Font** dialog box launcher to display the **Font** dialog box.

15. This is a tabbed dialog box, similar to those used in previous versions of *Word*. Click **Cancel** to close the **Font** dialog box.

16. Display the other basic tabs, one at a time, **Insert**, **Page Layout**, **References**, **Mailings**, **Review** and **View** to see which other commands are available.

17. Select the **Home** tab again.

18. Locate the **Quick Access Toolbar**.

19. Point at each button and read its **ToolTip**.

20. The third button is the **Repeat** button. This button has a dual function, it changes to a **Redo** button after the **Undo** button has been used.

21. To the right of the **Repeat** button is the **Customize Quick Access Toolbar** button, [=] . Click the button to display the menu.

Note: *To add commands not shown, click* **More Commands***. This displays the* **Word** **Options** *window with the* **Customize** *option selected.*

22. Click away from the menu to close it.

Exercise 36 - Exiting Word

Guidelines:

When *Word* is closed, if any documents are still open and have not been saved, a warning will be displayed with an option to save the changes.

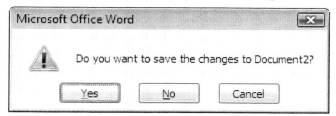

Actions:

1. Click the **Office Button**, , to reveal the drop down menu.

2. Place the mouse pointer over **Exit Word** and click once.

Note: *Word can also be closed by clicking the **Close** button,* ☒ *, in the top right corner of the screen.*

3. Select **No** if there is a prompt to save.

Section 5

Documents

By the end of this Section you should be able to:

Recognise the Layout of the Keyboard

Enter Text

Save Documents

Close Documents

Create New Documents

Open Existing Documents

Understand Document Views

Exercise 37 - The Keyboard

Guidelines:

There is only so much that can be done with the mouse, which is why computers also have a keyboard (*see example below*). The keyboard is basically the same as a normal typewriter keyboard (*1*), but there are extra keys. The top row contains the **Function Keys**: <F1> to <F12> (*3*). These keys are used to access shortcuts in some programs. On the main keyboard, the additional keys used most often are <**Ctrl**>, <**Alt**> (*left and right of 11*) and <**Enter**> (*9*).

At the far right of the keyboard is a numeric keypad (*6*), which also includes mathematical keys (**+**, **-**, etc.). Numbers can be entered more quickly using these keys. The **Number Lock** must be on to use this keypad - use the top left button on the numeric keypad (<**Num Lock**>) to switch it on or off.

To the left of the numeric keypad are directional keys, such as <**Home**>, <**Page Up**> (*15*) and arrow keys (*7*) that allow movement around a text document, for example. The <**Delete**> (*15*) and <**Backspace**> (*14*) keys are both used to delete text.

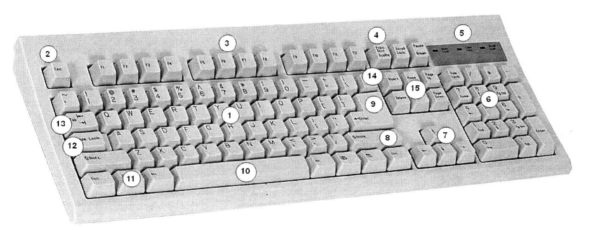

Keys on the diagram not already mentioned are: <**Esc**> (*2*) - the escape key, often an alternative to a **Cancel** option, <**Print Screen**> (*4*) - copies the exact content shown on screen, <**Shift**> (*8*) - hold this down to type a capital letter, or a symbol above another (e.g. **£** above the <**3**>). The <**Spacebar**> (*10*) adds one space to text, <**Caps Lock**> (*12*) switches to capitals until pressed again and <**Tab**> (*13*) moves along the page to the next **tab stop**, set at regular intervals to help line up text. The indicator lights (*5*) show if any locks are activated, such as <**Caps Lock**>.

Exercise 38 - Entering Text

Guidelines:

Any file created in *Word* is called a **document**. It can have one or several pages.

The keyboard is called an **input device** because it is used to input information to the computer. Any key pressed on the keyboard will appear in the document at the **Insertion Point**, where the cursor flashes. Each letter, number or symbol typed in is called a **character**.

Using <**Shift**> and the appropriate key will enter a capital letter. <**Caps Lock**> is used if a large amount of text is to be capitalised. Where there are two options on a key, then <**Shift**> should be used to enter the uppermost option.

Word uses a feature called **word wrap** when text is entered. This means that as you are typing, the end of a line is automatically detected and a new one started. <**Enter**> must be used in text entry to force a new line, i.e. to end a paragraph (this is known as a paragraph break). Pressing <**Enter**> without entering any text will create a blank line.

It is a common convention that there is one space between words and two spaces at the end of a sentence, although you should check what spacing is used where you work or study. Use <**Enter**> twice at the end of paragraphs, one to end the text and one to create a blank line. This will make the text easier to read.

Actions:

1.   Start *Word* so that there is a blank document in view. A flashing vertical bar called the **Insertion Point** is displayed indicating where on the screen text will be entered if a key is pressed. By default this is in the top left of the usable area of the page.

2.   Move the mouse pointer slowly over the screen.

Note: Double clicking will move the insertion point to the cursor position.

3.   Notice how a symbol appears next to the cursor. This indicates the alignment of the text. ⊥ means any text entered here will be aligned to the left, ≣ means the text will be centred and ≡⏋ means the text will be right aligned. Alignment will be explained in greater detail in section **10**.

*Note: Showing text alignment on the cursor is an option. It is controlled by the **Enable click and type** setting which can be accessed by clicking the **Office Button**, then selecting **Word Options | Advanced | Editing Options**.*

continued over

Exercise 38 - Continued

4. Enter the following text as fast as possible, ignoring any errors made. The text should appear at the **Insertion Point**. Use a double space between sentences.

> **A computer is an electronic machine that is automatically controlled; it can store a vast amount of information and works at fantastically high speeds. Computers do not have brains, humans who feed them information and program them to perform particular tasks do the thinking.**

Note: *Remember that during an examination, it is important to type carefully and accurately, so that the document is well presented, without any errors.*

5. Now press <**Enter**> to create new paragraph. This, by default should have a space to the paragraph above.

Note: *If there is not enough space between the paragraphs, press <**Enter**> again to create the space. Remember, this action creates an extra paragraph so when moving between paragraphs later you will have to use extra key presses.*

6. Continue entering text:

> **Computers can be used by individuals, or as part of a network. The largest computer network is the World Wide Web, which allows users to communicate with others and access information from all over the world.**

7. Click in front of the second sentence of this paragraph - **The largest computer network...** and then press <**Enter**>. This inserts a paragraph break, creating a new paragraph.

Note: *Jagged red lines may have appeared under words that are spelled incorrectly. Do not do anything about these yet, as editing and spell checking will be covered later.*

8. Leave this text on the screen for the next exercise.

Exercise 39 - Saving a New Document

Guidelines:

Text must be saved if it is to be used again. There are two main ways to save a document. **Save As** allows file name, file type and location to be specified and is therefore always used to save a newly created document, or to create a new copy. **Save** saves an existing file with the same name, location and type as it had before, therefore overwriting the original. You should be aware of where the data associated with this guide is located. The file you are about to save should be saved to the same location.

Actions:

1. Click the **Office Button** and select **Save As**. The **Save As** dialog box will appear. Use the **Navigation pane** to locate the supplied word processing data folder, **Unit 1 Word 2007 Data** (*see Note on Page 4*).

2. If the location of the folder is not as shown below, consult your tutor.

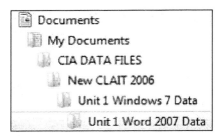

3. The document must be given a name. Enter **Computer Information** in the **File name** box (the highlighted text will automatically be deleted and the extension **.docx** will be added automatically).

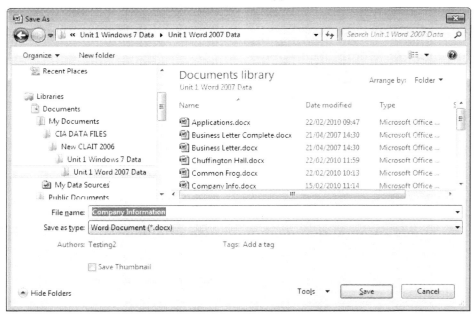

continued over

Exercise 39 - Continued

Note: A file name can be of any length. Choose a meaningful name but do not use any of the following characters: ><"*?:\ /;|.

4. Click the **Save** button, [Save], at the bottom right of the dialog box. The document is now saved with the name **Computer Information**. The new name of the document now appears in the **Title Bar**.

Company Information - Microsoft Word

5. At the bottom of the document, press <**Enter**> to create a new line and type in your name. Now there is a choice of saving methods. **Save As** will allow a new version of the document to be saved with a new name, or **Save** will update the existing version.

6. Click the **Save** button, on the **Quick Access Toolbar**. The updated version of the document is saved, overwriting the original.

7. Leave the document on the screen for the next exercise.

Note: When saving a new document for the first time, a name and location must be set. If you select **Save** for a new document, it will automatically display the **Save As** dialog box.

Exercise 40 - Closing a Document

Guidelines:

To clear all text from the screen and begin working on a new document, the current document can be closed. If the document has not been previously saved, or if it has been modified in any way, a prompt to save it will appear.

Actions:

1. The **Computer Information** document should still be present on the screen. At the bottom of the document, press **<Enter>** to create a new line and type in today's date in any format.

2. Now click the **Office Button** and choose the **Close** command. The message **Do you want to save the changes to "Computer Information"?** will appear on the screen.

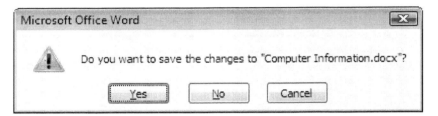

3. Select **Yes**. The document is automatically saved to the location specified earlier.

Note: *If the document has just been created and **Yes** is selected, the **Save As** dialog box will appear. **No** closes the document without saving and **Cancel** returns to the document.*

4. At this stage, the window should display an empty grey area below the **Ribbon**. Try typing in some text. Nothing happens because there are no documents open at the moment.

Exercise 41 - Creating a New Document

Guidelines:

Further new documents can be created at any time within *Word*. The **New Document** dialog box provides several options for creating documents. They may be created from scratch, or preset templates can be used to help create standard documents such as letters and faxes, etc.

Actions:

1. Click the **Office Button** and click New. The **New Document** dialog box appears.

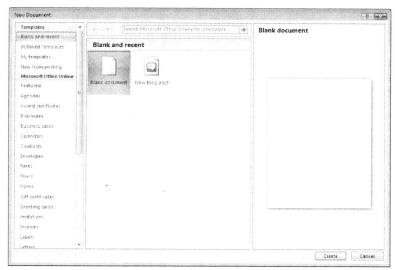

2. Make sure **Blank document** is selected and click the **Create** button and a new document will instantly be displayed on the screen. Until it is saved and given a name, new documents will be called Document 1 or Document 2, etc. depending on how many documents have been created in this session.

3. Enter the following text, do not worry about mistakes yet.

> **Recent research has questioned previous findings that coffee is detrimental to health. It has been suggested that moderate coffee consumption can help prevent some forms of cancer and, in heavy drinkers, can help avert cirrhosis of the liver. This should encourage workers to drink more coffee; not only does it keep you alert, but it can help safeguard you against some serious diseases.**

4. Click the **Office Button** and select **Save As** to save the document in the word processing data folder, using the file name **Coffee**. Click **Save**.

5. Click the **Office Button** again and select **Close** to clear the document from the screen.

Exercise 42 - Opening an Existing Document

Guidelines:

Once a document has been created and saved, it can be opened at any time.

Actions:

1. The text area of the screen should be clear from the end of the previous exercise. Click the **Office Button** and select **Open** to display the **Open** dialog box.

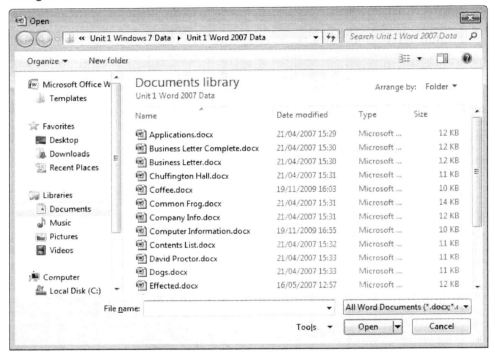

2. The **Unit 1 Word 2007 Data** folder is displayed as it was the last visited folder. Scroll down, select the file **Grand Canyon** and then click **Open**.

3. Click the **Office Button** and select **Close** to close the document, then click the **Office Button** again. The most recent documents that have been used by *Word* are listed at the right.

4. Click once on the file name **Computer Information** to open the file.

5. Close it again.

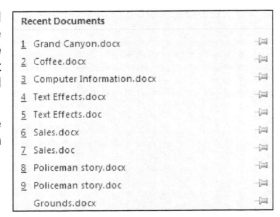

Not needed

Exercise 43 - Views

Guidelines:

When working in *Word* there are different ways to view a document. The most commonly used are **Draft** view and **Print Layout** view. In **Draft** view, the document is shown in its basic format. In **Print Layout** view, the document margins can be seen. The document is shown exactly as it will appear when it is printed.

Actions:

1. From the data files supplied, open the document **Dogs**. This document has been saved in **Print Layout View**.

2. The views are changed either by using the **View** tab on the **Ribbon** or the **Views** buttons on the right hand side of the **Status Bar**. To change the view, click the **View** tab.

3. To change to **Draft** view click **Draft**. The other buttons are used to display more views. **Full Screen Reading**, if displayed has to be closed using the **Close** button, top right.

4. Display the **Home** tab.

5. To change the view quickly, without using the **Ribbon**, select the appropriate button from the bottom right corner of the screen.

6. Change to **Draft** view by selecting **View** and clicking **Draft**.

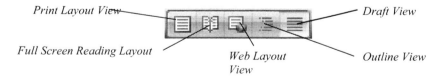

Print Layout View — Full Screen Reading Layout — Web Layout View — Draft View — Outline View

Note: The **View** buttons are always displayed, except for **Full Reading**, which has to be closed. The **View** buttons are therefore easier to use than the **View** tab on the **Ribbon**.

7. Change back to **Print Layout** view by selecting the **Print Layout** view button, ▣.

8. Close the document.

Exercise 44 - Revision

1. Start a new document.

2. Start with the title **Personal Profile**.

3. Type in two paragraphs of text about yourself and the main duties your job involves (or about the course you are studying).

4. Save the document as **Personal** and close it.

Exercise 45 - Revision

1. Open the document **Dogs**.

2. How many methods are there to open a file from within *Word*?

3. How do you find the **Open** option?

4. How many recently opened documents are usually listed on the **Office Button** menu?

5. Change the view of **Dogs** to **Draft** view.

6. Where is the button located to make this change?

7. Has this changed the document at all?

8. Close **Dogs**.

9. Start a **New** document.

10. Describe the method you used to do this.

11. Type in the following text, you will correct any errors later. Replace #### with words of your own

> **Holidays cannot come quickly enough for me. I wish I was able to take more than one a year, but that would mean more expense and I just can't afford it.**
>
> **The next holiday I am taking will be to ####. I am really looking forward to it, but I wish it were next week instead of next month. I can't wait to #### and ####.**

12. Save the document as **Holidays** and then close it.

*Note: Check the **Answers** section at the end of the guide.*

Section 6

Editing Text

By the end of this Section you should be able to:

Move around using the Mouse and Cursor Keys
Insert and Delete Text

Exercise 46 - Using the Mouse

Guidelines:

The mouse provides an easy way of moving around a document. Although small movements are normally made using the keyboard, the mouse and scroll bars are used to move to a different area. To move to a particular place on the document, simply point and click.

The usual method of moving around the screen is by a combination of key presses and mouse movements.

Actions:

1. Open the document **Company Info**. Change to **Draft** view.

2. The scroll bar arrows are used to move around a document from left to right or up and down.

3. Click once on the down arrow at the right edge of the document and text moves up by a small amount.

4. Click once on the up arrow at the right edge of the document and text moves down by a small amount.

5. Click on the scroll button and while holding the mouse button down, drag the button to the bottom of the scroll bar (as the text does not go to the bottom of the page, it may not want to stay there, however, the last line of text is always on view).

continued over

Exercise 46 - Continued

6. Change back to **Print Layout View**. The scroll button appears to be much bigger. This is because there is less scrolling to do. Click and drag the scroll button until you can see the bottom of the page.

7. Change back to **Draft View**. Move the scroll button to the bottom of the document again.

8. Click on the scroll <u>bar</u> above the button to move up the screen to the top of the document.

9. Experiment with the scroll bar, buttons and arrows.

10. None of this change of view has moved the insertion point. It is still at the beginning of the document – unless you have accidentally clicked within the document.

11. Move the cursor, I to the end of the second paragraph …**their requirements.** Click once and the insertion point now flashes where you clicked. Text could now be entered here.

12. Practise moving the cursor around the screen. You can even click in the middle of words.

13. Close the document.

Exercise 47 - Cursor Movement

Guidelines:

The cursor keys can be used to move the cursor character by character and line by line. Some of the more useful movement keys are as follows:

Description	Key Press	Description	Key Press
Beginning of a line	<Home>	Beginning of next paragraph	<Ctrl ↓>
End of a line	<End>	Up one paragraph	<Ctrl ↑>
Beginning of a document	<Ctrl Home>	Next word	<Ctrl →>
End of a document	<Ctrl End>	Previous word	<Ctrl ←>

Note: *The quickest way to move the cursor around the screen is to position the mouse and click the left button.*

Where two keys are mentioned, hold down the first key, while pressing and releasing the second.

Actions:

1. Open the document **Applications** for this exercise.

2. Move the cursor to the end of the first line by pressing **<End>**.

3. Move down a paragraph using **<Ctrl ↓>**. Remember every time you press the **<Enter>** key a new paragraph is formed.

4. Move to the end of the document using **<Ctrl End>**.

5. Move to the beginning of the document using **<Ctrl Home>**.

6. Press **<Ctrl →>** to move to the beginning of the next word. Continue using this key press until you are on the next line.

7. Press **<Ctrl ←>** until you are back at the beginning.

8. Close the document <u>without</u> saving any changes.

Exercise 48 - Inserting and Deleting Text

Guidelines:

Both the mouse and the cursor keys can be used to move the insertion point. Mistakes can be erased, or text inserted wherever required.

Actions:

1. Open the document **Chuffington Hall**.

2. Identify the **Backspace** key. It is above the **Enter** key and usually has a ← on the key. Characters to the left of the cursor are deleted by pressing the <**Backspace**> key.

3. Identify the **Delete** key. It is situated in a group of keys above the arrow keys and has **Delete** on it. Characters to the right of the cursor are deleted using the <**Delete**> key.

4. Click in the word **eleven** in the second sentence of the first paragraph. Delete the word **eleven** using the <**Backspace**> and/or <**Delete**> keys.

Note:	*Either the <**Backspace**> or the <**Delete**> key can be used to delete text. They are both useful for deleting characters or odd words, but are slow if used to delete larger amounts of text. This is why Word has quick ways of selecting large areas of text, covered in Section 8.*

5. In its place, type in **twelve**.

6. Make the following alterations to the document, by inserting and deleting text as necessary: first paragraph, first sentence: change **Hall** to **Manor**.

7. Second paragraph, first sentence: insert a space in **eachcase**.

8. Second paragraph, first sentence: change **wood stolen** to **wood has been stolen**.

9. Third paragraph, last sentence: change **continues** to **is continuing**.

10. Save the document as **Solved**.

11. Close the document.

Exercise 49 - Revision

1. Open the document **Applications**.

2. Move the scroll button to view the bottom of the document. In which direction did you drag the button? You could have used the scroll arrow, what other method could you have used?

3. You are viewing the bottom of the document. What key press will place the insertion point here? Use it.

4. Use the mouse to place the insertion point at the beginning of the last paragraph. Insert the following text:

    You can produce documents, booklets, magazines and newspapers using a

5. Insert a space after the last word entered.

6. Delete the following text from the remainder of the sentence using either backspace or delete:

    are used to produce documents, booklets, magazines, newspapers etc.

7. Delete the **s** from **programs**. The sentence should now read:

    You can produce documents, booklets, magazines and newspapers using a Desktop publishing program.

8. Close the document. At the dialog box select **No**. This closes the document <u>without</u> saving the changes.

*Note: Check the **Answers** section at the end of the guide.*

Exercise 50 - Revision

1. Open the document **Grounds**.

2. Save the document as **Grounds2**.

3. You are now to correct the errors made in this document.

4. Use the **Backspace** or **Delete** keys to erase any errors. Enter any corrections.

5. Save the file with the same name by using the **Save** button, .

6. Close the document.

Section 7

Printing

By the end of this Section you should be able to:

Print Preview a Document

Change Page Setup and Orientation

Print a Document

Exercise 51 - Previewing a Document

Guidelines:

It is important to make sure a document looks as you expect it to before printing it. **Print Preview** shows the layout of the document.

Actions:

1.   Open the document **Dogs**.

2.   To preview the document, click the **Office Button**, move the cursor over **Print** and select **Print Preview** from the list.

3.   Position the cursor over the page until it becomes 🔍.

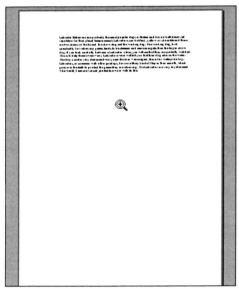

4.   Click the mouse to zoom into the page. The pointer now becomes 🔍. Click once to zoom out.

5.   The magnification of a document can be adjusted using the **Zoom Control**, [49% ⊖ ▭ ━━━ ⊕], situated on the right of the **Status Bar**. Drag the slider to approximately **148%** change the magnification.

6.   Use the **Zoom Control** to change the magnification to **50%**.

Note: *The **Zoom** button,* [Zoom], *displays a dialog box which can be used to control the zoom process.*

7.   Click [Close Print Preview], but leave the document open for the next exercise.

Exercise 52 - Page Setup

Guidelines:

Page Setup is used to change margins, i.e. how much white space appears around the text, when printed. The **orientation** of the page can be changed, from portrait to landscape, or landscape to portrait (see the images in the **Orientation** area in the dialog box below).

Actions:

1. The document **Dogs** should be open from the previous exercise. Select the **Page Layout** tab and click the **Page Setup** dialog box launcher, ▣, to display the **Page Setup** dialog box.

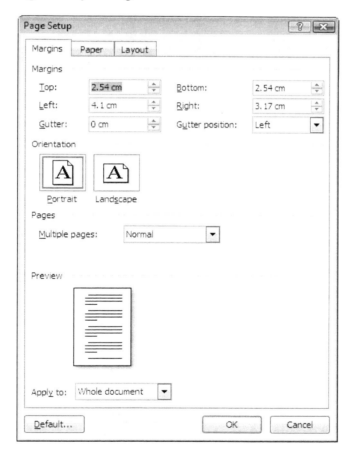

2. Make sure the **Margins** tab is selected. Use the spinner buttons ▣ to change the **Top** margin to **5 cm**.

3. Because you had to use so many clicks to do this, it is not the quickest way to make a big change. It is easier to edit the number. Click and drag across **4.1 cm** in the **Left** margin box. It becomes highlighted.

continued over

Exercise 52 - Continued

4.   Enter the number **5**. This has now replaced the original number.

5.   Repeat for the **Right** margin and click **OK**.

6.   **Print Preview** the document. It is shown with the new margin settings.

7.   The commands are still available in this view. Click the **Margins** button and select **Custom Margins**. The top margin is highlighted, enter **6** in the box. The number is replaced.

8.   Press the <**Tab**> key, [icon]. This moves the selection to the next margin (bottom). You <u>do not</u> want to change this one.

9.   Press <**Tab**> again. Change the left and right margins to **6**.

10. Click **OK** and observe the result in the preview.

11. Close **Print Preview**.

12. On the **Page Layout** tab, click [Orientation].

13. From the drop down list, select **Landscape**.

14. Check **Print Preview** to see the changes.

15. Close **Print Preview**.

16. Change the orientation back to **Portrait**.

17. Leave the **Dogs** document open for the next exercise.

Exercise 53 - Printing a Document

Guidelines:

Once a document has been previewed it is ready to be printed.

Actions:

1. Use the **Dogs** document, which should still be open from the previous exercise.

2. The easiest way to print is to use the **Print** button, 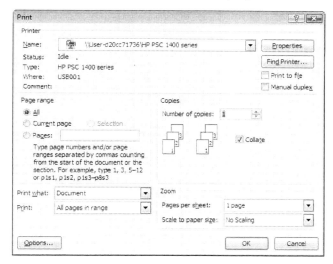 from the **Microsoft Office** list. A single copy of the entire document will be printed, whether it has one page or one hundred pages. Click the **Office Button** and move the mouse over the arrow at the right of the **Print** button. Select **Quick Print** to print the document.

3. Change the top and side margins to **3 cm** each, then **Print Preview** the document. Close **Print Preview**.

4. Click the **Office Button** and select **Print** to display the **Print** dialog box.

*Your **Print** dialog box depends on the specific printer and may not be exactly the same as the one shown.*

5. Notice that the highlight is in the **Number of copies** box. This can be changed using the spinner buttons or by overtyping the number. Leave the number as 1 and click on **OK**. This will print one copy of the document with the new margins.

6. Close the document <u>without</u> saving any changes.

*Note: Documents can also be printed from **Print Preview** using the **Print** button.*

Exercise 54 - Revision

1. Open the document **Applications**.

2. **Print Preview** the document.

3. Change the **Zoom** to **100%**.

4. Use the **Print** button to print the document from within the preview.

5. Display the **Page Setup** dialog box and change all the margins to **4 cm**.

6. Close **Print Preview** and **Print** the document again.

7. Close the document <u>without</u> saving.

Exercise 55 - Revision

1. Open the document **Company Info**.

2. **Print Preview** the document.

3. Change the orientation to **Landscape**.

4. **Print** a copy of the document.

5. Close it <u>without</u> saving.

Exercise 56 - Revision

1. Open the document **David Proctor**.

2. In the second sentence, change **Social Science** to **Social Studies**.

3. Use the keypad to go to the end of the document. Press <**Enter**> to make a new paragraph. Add the following text:

   In the future I hope to own my own company, probably staying in car sales, but I remain open minded and optimistic.

4. **Print Preview** your file. Make sure it all fits on one page.

5. **Print** it out.

6. Close the file <u>saving</u> the change made.

Section 8

Formatting Text

By the end of this Section you should be able to:

Select Words and Sentences

Select Lines and Paragraphs

Use Underline, Bold and Italic

Change Text Fonts

Change Text Size

Cut, Copy and Paste Text

Move Text

Apply Bullets and Numbers

Insert a Table

Apply Borders and Shading

Exercise 57 - Selecting Words and Sentences

Guidelines:

Most features of *Word* work on the basis that text is first selected and then an action, deleting for example, is performed upon the selected text. There are various ways to select text - use the method you prefer. Once you are able to select text correctly, creating documents will become much quicker.

Actions:

1.   Open the document **Applications**.

2.   Text can be selected by clicking and dragging the mouse. In the first paragraph, select the final word, **car**, by clicking at the beginning of the word and, holding down the mouse button, drag to the end of the word before releasing the mouse.

3.   **Car** is highlighted to show that it has been selected. Now delete it by pressing <**Delete**>.

4.   It is easier to select a word by double clicking on it. Double click on **particular**, which is now the last word in the first paragraph and delete it.

5.   Now select the first sentence in the document by clicking and dragging.

6.   To remove the text selection, click once, away from the selected text.

Note: *Once text is selected, if any key is pressed, the selected text will be deleted and replaced with the key press. Be careful - always remove the selection before pressing keys.*

7.   An easy way to select a sentence is to hold down the <**Ctrl**> key and click anywhere within the sentence. Select the first sentence of the second paragraph using this method.

8.   Delete the selected text.

9.   The cursor keys can be used together with the <**Shift**> key to select text. Position the cursor at the beginning of the text.

10.   Hold down <**Shift**> and press → several times. This selects the text character by character – this includes spaces.

11.   As you know, <**Ctrl** →> moves the cursor word by word, so combined with <**Shift**> it selects word by word.

12.   Test this by holding down both <**Shift**> and <**Ctrl**> and using → to make a selection. Click away to remove the selection.

13.   Close the document without saving, so recent changes are lost.

IGNORE

Exercise 58 - Selecting Lines and Paragraphs

Guidelines:

The **Selection Bar**, an invisible area at the left margin of the page, is used to select larger areas of text.

Actions:

1. Open the document **Applications** again. This exercise is easier in **Print Layout View**. Change to that view now, if necessary.

2. Move the mouse pointer towards the left margin until it changes to ⇗. This is the **selection arrow**.

3. Move the mouse to the first paragraph, making sure the selection arrow is still visible and click once to select a line of text.

4. Click again, away from the margin, to remove the selection.

5. At the left of the first paragraph, display the selection arrow again. This time, double click the mouse to select the whole paragraph.

6. Remove the selection and display the selection arrow again.

7. Click at the beginning of the first paragraph and, holding down the mouse button, move down the margin until two paragraphs are highlighted.

A database is a vast store of information consisting of records. A record contains information relating to one person or one company and is made up of individual pieces of information called fields. For example, you may create your records with the following fields: company name, address, telephone number, credit limit, amount owed, payment due, etc. When all the information has been entered, the database can be used to search for particular information. This is called cross-referencing and allows you, for example, to find out at the end of the month who the company owes money to and how much, in order to settle accounts. New information can be entered and the database is updated to include the new data, so that it is always up to date. The computer operated by the DVLA in Swansea (Driving Vehicle Licensing Authority) is an example of a large database. Information relating to every motor vehicle in the U.K. is stored on computer. This information can be accessed to find out who owns a particular car.

In word processing, a computer behaves like an advanced form of typewriter. Facilities are provided for entering, manipulating, storing and retrieving blocks of text. This means that standard letters and lists of names and addresses can be generated separately, then letters to everyone on the list can be printed without the need to retype the document. The computer retrieves the letter and the first name and address, prints the letter, retrieves the next name and address, changes the information in the letter, prints the next letter and so on. This feature is known as Mail Merge.

8. To select the entire document, click three times in rapid succession, in the **Selection Bar**.

9. Now press <**Delete**>. The whole document is deleted.

10. Close the document without saving any changes.

Exercise 59 - Underline, Bold and Italic

Guidelines:

The **Underline**, **Bold** and **Italic** features allow text to be emphasised, so it stands out on the page. Although text can be formatted as it is typed, a more efficient way is to enter text first, then format it later.

Actions:

1.   Open the document **Grand Canyon**.

2.   Select the first paragraph and click the **Italic** button, *I*, on the **Font** group of the **Home** tab. All the text will be in italics (sloping to the right).

3.   Now select the second paragraph and click the **Bold** button, **B**.

4.   Underline the third paragraph using the **Underline** button, <u>U</u>.

5.   The last paragraph is to have all three effects added to it. Select the paragraph. Rather than click each button in turn, click the **Font** dialog box launcher to open the **Font** dialog box.

6.   Many changes can now be made at the same time. In **Font style**, click on **Bold Italic**. From **Underline style**, choose the first line option.

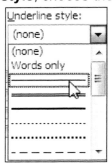

7.   Click **OK**.

8.   **Print Preview** the document, then print a copy of the document.

9.   Leave the document open for the next exercise.

Exercise 60 - Fonts

Guidelines:

A font is a type or style of print. There are two different types of font: **serif** and **sans serif**. A serif font, e.g. Times New Roman, Book Antiqua, has extra lines or curls on the 'stalk' of the letters (q); a sans serif font, e.g. Arial, Comic Sans MS, Tahoma, does not (q). A combination of the software in use and the selected printer determines which fonts are available for use.

Note: To change the font of a single word, position the cursor within the word and choose the required font.

Actions:

1. Use the **Grand Canyon** document. This document has been created using a different font.

2. Select the whole of the document.

3. The quickest way to change a font is via the **Font** box, in the **Font** group on the **Home** tab. Click the drop down arrow at the right of the box to display the list of available fonts.

4. Notice when you drop the list down, how the name of the font is displayed in that font to give you idea of how your text will look. Also as the cursor moves over a font in the list, the highlighted text in the document shows that font.

5. Scroll through the list and select **Garamond**.

Note: If any of these fonts are unavailable, then select an alternative.

6. Select the first paragraph, then click the **Font** dialog box launcher.

7. Use the **Font** list to change the font of this paragraph to **Arial** and click **OK**.

8. Print the document out again and compare with the print out from the previous exercise.

9. Close the document <u>without</u> saving.

Exercise 61 - Changing the Size of Text

Guidelines:

The size of printed text can be changed either before or after the text is typed. The range of sizes available will be determined by a combination of the printer, software and font in use. Size is defined in **points** (pt) - the larger the point size, the larger the character appears.

Actions:

1. Open the document **Dogs**.

2. Select the first sentence.

3. Click the drop down arrow at the right of the **Font Size** box, located in the **Font** group on the **Home** tab, to display a list of sizes.

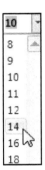

4. Select size **14pt** and the size of the selected text increases.

5. Place the cursor within the word **yellow** in the second sentence and change its size to **18pt**. Remember single words do not have to be selected to be changed.

6. Increase the size of **chocolate** in the same sentence to **24pt**.

> Labrador Retrievers are probably the most popular dogs in Britain and have a well-deserved reputation for their placid temperament. Labradors can be black,
>
> **yellow** or **chocolate** and there are two strains of the breed: the show dog and the working dog. The working dog, bred specifically for retrieving game, tends to be slimmer and more energetic than the larger show dog. If you look carefully between a Labrador's toes, you will see that they are partially webbed. This is to help them swim – any Labrador owner will tell you that their dog adores the water. The dog's coat is very dense and waxy near the skin – once again, this is for waterproofing. Labradors, in common with other gundogs, have a rubbery kind of flap in their mouth, which goes over the teeth to protect the game they are retrieving. The Labrador is a very loyal animal who would, I am convinced, protect its owner with its life.

7. Select the final sentence and change it to **48pt**. You may have to use the scroll bar at the right side of the size list to reach 48.

8. **Print Preview** the document to see the result, then print a copy. Change to **Draft** view.

9. Select the whole document, then click the **Font** dialog box launcher.

10. Use the **Font Size** box to change the text to **16pt** and the font to **Arial**. Click **OK**.

11. Print out one copy.

12. Save the document as **Resized** and close it.

Exercise 62 - Cut, Copy and Paste

Guidelines:

The **Cut, Copy** and **Paste** commands allow text to be moved around a document, from one place to another, quickly and easily. When text is cut, it is removed from its original location; when copied, the original is untouched.

When copied or cut, text is placed in a temporary storage area known as the **Clipboard**. Up to **24** cut or copied items can be held on the **Clipboard**.

Actions:

1. Open the document **Grand Canyon**.

2. Highlight the second paragraph and click the **Cut** button, in the **Clipboard** group of the **Home** tab on the **Ribbon**.

3. Move the cursor to the beginning of the last paragraph and click the **Paste** button, to place the cut text at the insertion point. A **Smart Tag**, appears giving further pasting options. Ignore it for now.

4. Select the first sentence, **Around six million years ago....**.

5. Click the **Clipboard** launcher (shown in the diagram on the right). This opens the **Clipboard Task Pane**, allowing selections to be made from the entries.

6. Click the **Copy** button, . Every time a cut or a copy is made, an icon representing it is added to the **Clipboard**, with a few lines of text to help identify the item.

7. The copied text is placed on the **Clipboard**, above the first item. Filling the **Clipboard** in this way is known as **Collect and Paste**.

8. At the end of the document, press **<Enter>** to start a new paragraph, then click the **Around six million...** item in the **Clipboard**. This will paste this text at the end of the document. Notice how the original text is untouched.

9. The **Clipboard** will now remain on the side of the document until it is closed.

Note: Paste All *on the* **Task Pane** *pastes all items held there and* Clear All *clears the* **Clipboard**.

Exercise 63 - Moving and Copying Text

Guidelines:

The **Drag and Drop** facility speeds up the process of moving text from one location to another within a document. It is best used to move small amounts of text, cut and paste works better with larger areas.

Actions:

1. The document **Grand Canyon**, should already be open, if not open it.

2. Close the **Clipboard** using the **Close** button, top right of the task pane.

3. Select the first sentence and move the mouse over the text until it becomes an arrow.

> Around six million years ago, the Colorado River in Arizona, U.S. began to carve a gorge through the landscape. That gorge became what we know today as the Grand Canyon. The Canyon is around 217 miles long, over a mile deep and 4 miles wide at its

4. Click and hold down the mouse button, then drag the mouse to the end of

    the text. As the text is being dragged, the cursor becomes ▨ and the **Status Bar** reads **Move to where?**. A dashed vertical line appears where the text will be inserted.

5. Release the mouse to drop the text at the end of the document.

Note: *The drag and drop feature becomes drag and copy if the* **<Ctrl>** *key is held*

    down whilst the text is being dragged. The cursor appears as ▨ *and the* **Status Bar** *reads* **Copy to where?**

6. Select the sentence that has just been moved.

7. Hold down **<Ctrl>** and drag to the beginning of the text before releasing the mouse.

8. The text is copied to the beginning of the document. **Print** the document.

9. Practise moving and copying within this document using this technique.

10. Close the document <u>without</u> saving.

Exercise 64 - Bullets and Numbering

Guidelines:

Lists and paragraphs can automatically be numbered or bulleted. In each case, a hanging indent is also applied. This separates the text from the numbering and improves the appearance of the document.

If an item is removed from the list, the remaining items are automatically renumbered.

Actions:

1. Open the document **Grand Canyon**.

2. Select all of the text.

3. Number the paragraphs by clicking the **Numbering** button, , on the **Paragraph** group.

4. Delete paragraph number **3**, referring to the **Colorado Plateau**. Notice how the remaining paragraphs are renumbered.

5. Print the document.

6. With all of the paragraphs selected, click the **Bullets** button, , to bullet them.

7. Print the document.

8. Close it <u>without</u> saving the changes.

9. Start a new document.

10. Enter a list of five first names, each one on a new line.

11. Select the list and apply bullets.

12. Change the bullets to numbers.

13. Remove one of the names in the middle of the list. The remaining names are renumbered.

14. Print the document.

15. Close the document <u>without</u> saving.

Exercise 65 - Inserting a Table

Guidelines:

The table feature makes it easy to create documents, such as invoices, that have a tabular format. Tables provide a more effective way of presenting tabular data than tabs and allow that data to be manipulated more easily. Tables consist of rows, running from top to bottom and columns running from left to right, to create cells as in spreadsheets.

Once a table has been created, it is simple to enter text and move around within it. It is probably easier to type the text into the table first and then to format it, i.e. correct column widths, etc.

Actions:

1. Start a new document.

2. To create a table, select the **Insert** tab and click the **Table** button, When the grid appears, click and drag on the grid until **4x4 Table** is displayed.

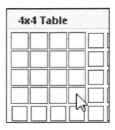

3. Release the mouse button. A table of 4 columns by 4 rows is created.

4. The insertion point will be flashing inside the first cell.

Note: Use <**Tab**> to move forward in a table and <**Shift Tab**> to move backwards. The cursor can also be positioned in the required cell by clicking. When entering text, do not use <**Enter**> unless a new line is required within the same cell, e.g. as in an address.

5. Enter the following text into the table:

Company	Share Price	Sector	Type of Business
Global	1240	Chemicals	PetroChemicals
Biro Bank	300	Banking	Corporate Finance
Sparkys	130	Stores	Electrical Retailer

6. Save the document as **Table**.

7. Leave the document open.

Exercise 66 - Applying Borders and Shading

Guidelines:

Borders can be added to individual cells, to a range of cells, or to a whole table. Gridlines are non-printing guides surrounding cells; however, a grid border can be applied to a table that follows the gridlines. Shading can be used to enhance the appearance of a table or to draw attention to a particular cell. However, it is important not to overdo borders and shading, to ensure the document can be easily read.

Actions:

1. Using the document from the previous exercise, select the whole table (click anywhere in the table and click the **Move table** icon at the top left, ⊞), then click the **Borders** button drop down, on the **Design** tab, in the **Table Styles** group.

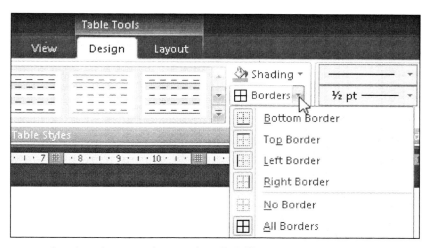

2. To remove the borders and see the **Gridlines**, select **No Border**. These lines are only there to act as a guide; they will not be seen when the page is printed.

3. Preview the document and notice no gridlines are shown.

4. Close **Print Preview**.

5. The table should still be selected, if not, select it.

6. Select the **Layout** tab, under **Table Tools** and select **View Gridlines** to turn the gridlines off. Click **View Gridlines** to display them again.

7. Select the top row of the table by clicking in the selection bar at the left of the first row, then click the **Borders** button drop down.

continued over

Exercise 66 - Continued

8. Select **Borders and Shading** to display the **Borders and Shading** dialog box.

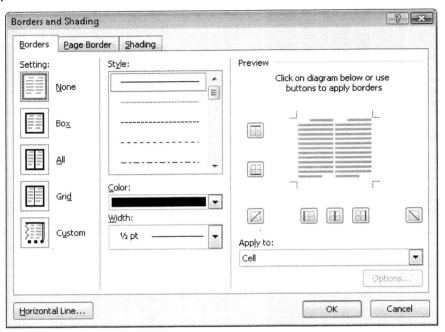

9. Select **Box** from the **Setting** area, select a double line **Style**, and a **Color** of red (notice the **Apply to** area shows **Cell**).

*Note: The buttons in the **Preview** area can be used to apply borders.*

10. Click **OK**. The border is applied to the selected cells, i.e. around the top row.

11. Click in the **Share Price** cell to select it then click the **Shading** button drop down.

12. Choose a pale aqua colour (as shown opposite).

13. Click on another cell to see the effect of the shading.

14. Shade the remainder of the top row with the same colour.

15. Select the rest of the table (click and drag down the left side) and shade it with any pale colour.

16. Experiment further with shading.

17. Close the document <u>without</u> saving.

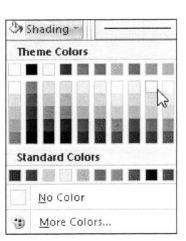

Exercise 67 - Revision

1. Open the document **Text Effects**.

2. You are directed to change the font and effects of each sentence. The first one is done for you as an example. Do this now. Notice that the **Wingdings** font is a series of pictures rather than letters.

3. Save the document as **Text Effects2**.

4. **Print Preview** the document.

5. **Print** the document then close it.

Exercise 68 - Revision

1. Open the document **Common Frog**. If any of the fonts mentioned are not available use an alternative.

2. Underline the title and make it bold. Increase the font size to **14pt**.

3. Change the font of the first paragraph to **Tahoma**.

4. Change the font of the second paragraph to **Monotype Corsiva**, decrease the size to **10pt**.

5. Change the font of the third paragraph to **Book Antiqua** and the size to **12pt**.

6. Change the font of the final paragraph to **Courier New** and make it **Italic**.

7. **Move** the second paragraph to the end of the document.

8. **Print Preview** the document and print a copy.

9. Close the document <u>without</u> saving.

Exercise 69 - Revision

1. In a new document, make a list of about five friends, entering the surname first.

2. Use **Cut** and **Paste** to arrange them in alphabetical order.

3. Save the document as **Friends**.

4. **Copy** all of the text and paste underneath the existing text.

5. Apply numbers to the entire list.

6. Delete the last 5 names. Use **Cut** and **Paste** to sort the remaining names in descending alphabetical order.

7. Insert a 2x5 table (2 columns, 5 rows).

8. Use drag and drop to <u>copy</u> a name to each cell in the first column- they don't have to be in any particular order. The table text will also be numbered.

9. Shade alternate rows in the table with pale blue.

10. Save the changes to the document and close it.

11. Open and **Clear** the **Clipboard** and **Close** it using the **Close** button, ⊠, at the top right of the **Task Pane**.

Exercise 70 - Revision

1. Open the document **Effected**. Ignore the instructions at the top of the document.

2. Change the **margins** in **Page Setup** to **4 cm** each for the **Top**, **Left** and **Right** margins.

3. Move the paragraph that uses **Arial** to the end of the text. Adjust the spacing of this newly placed paragraph by using <**Enter**>.

4. Display the **Clipboard** and cut the paragraph that uses the **Comic Sans** font.

5. Copy the paragraph that uses the **Book Antiqua** font.

6. Paste the **Comic Sans** paragraph so that it appears before the last paragraph.

7. Clear the **Clipboard** and **Close** it.

8. Adjust all line spacing so that there is one blank line between paragraphs.

9. Save the document as **Effected2** and print a copy of the document.

10. Close the document.

Section 9

Tools

By the end of this Section you should be able to:

Check Spelling and Grammar

Search for Text

Replace Text

Use Word Count

Exercise 71 - Automatic Spell Checking

Guidelines:

Word can check the text you enter against its own large dictionary. Words not in the dictionary can be added but you will not need to do this. There are two main ways of spell checking. <u>Either</u> spell check while typing, <u>or</u> use the **Spelling Checker**. Unrecognised words are shown with a wavy red line underneath. Green wavy lines refer to grammatical errors.

Actions:

1. Open the document **Policeman Story**. For now, ignore grammatical errors.

2. If there are red and green wavy lines beneath some of the text, then the **Automatic Spelling & Grammar** feature is turned on. **Move to Step 6**. If not, continue following the steps.

3. Click the **Office Button** and click **Word Options**. Click **Proofing** at the left.

4. Under **When correcting spelling and grammar in Word**, **Check spelling as you type** should have a check mark against it, as should **Mark grammar errors as you type** and **Check grammar with spelling**. If they don't, just click in the appropriate white box to insert the tick.

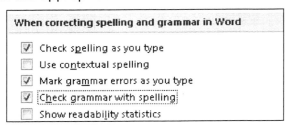

5. Click **OK** to close the **Word Options** window.

6. The quickest way of correcting errors is by using the mouse. Place the mouse over the first item underlined in red, **aproached** and click with the <u>right</u> mouse button. A shortcut menu appears. Alternative spelling suggestions are given in a list, in this case there is only one suggestion, or the suggestions may be ignored.

7. Click with the <u>left</u> mouse button to select the correct spelling. The error is corrected.

8. When text is being entered, a **Spell Book** is shown in the **Status Bar** indicating the current status of the document. If there are mistakes, appears, if everything is correct, appears.

9. Continue to correct the spelling errors. One is not a spelling error, but a repeated word, **saw saw**. Select **Delete Repeated Word**.

10. Print the document and close it <u>without</u> saving.

Exercise 72 - Spell Checker

Guidelines:

Another way to check spelling is to use the **Spelling and Grammar** dialog box.

Actions:

1. Open the document **Policeman Story** again. Make the title **Unexplained** bold.

2. Spelling errors are underlined in red and grammatical errors in green. Place the cursor at the beginning of the document, select the **Review** tab and click the **Spelling and Grammar** button. The **Spelling and Grammar** dialog box appears. Ignore any grammatical errors by clicking **Ignore Once**.

3. The first spelling error is shown in the top area. Suggested alternatives are shown beneath. Errors can be ignored, changed or added to the dictionary. Select the alternative **approached** and click **Change**.

4. Work through the document, making corrections as necessary. **Ignore** the green grammatical errors for the moment. The following message appears when the check is complete.

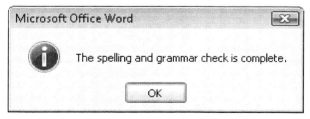

5. Click **OK** and save the document as **Explained** before closing it.

*Note: If the word required does not appear in the **Suggestions** box, it may be typed into the upper area of the **Spelling and Grammar** dialog box, correcting the error, and then clicking **Change**.*

Exercise 73 - Grammar Checker

Guidelines:

Grammar is also checked as text is entered. *Word* makes suggestions which, like spelling suggestions, can be accepted or ignored.

Actions:

1.   Open the document **Sales**.

2.   The grammatical errors are underlined in green (it may take a few seconds for the errors to appear after the file is opened, if they don't appear quickly, double click at the end of the document). Click the **Spelling and Grammar** button from the **Review** tab.

3.   Notice how the buttons at the right of the dialog box are slightly different to when spelling is checked. Click **Next Sentence**.

4.   The second error finds an extra space before the **?**. Click **Change** to accept the suggestion.

5.   The third error is a little trickier in that a full stop has mistakenly been placed in the middle of a sentence. Choose **Ignore Once**, but remember where it is. Move the dialog box, if necessary, to view the error.

6.   Click **OK** when the grammar check is complete.

7.   Go back to the full stop error and delete it. Check that the **Spell Book** is showing all complete, ![icon] .

8.   Save the document as **Corrected** and close it.

Note: It is good practice to proof read a document, even after it has been spell and grammar checked.

Exercise 74 - Searching a Document

Guidelines:

Visually searching for a word or phrase in a document can be tedious. The **Find** command moves directly to a specific word or group of characters.

Actions:

1. Open the document **Applications**.

2. Click **Find** from the **Editing** group on the **Home** tab to display the **Find and Replace** dialog box.

3. On the **Find** tab, in the **Find what** box, enter **information** and then click **Find Next**. The first occurrence of the word is highlighted, A database is a vast store of **information**.

4. Click **Find Next** again to move to the next occurrence.

5. In this way, find all occurrences of the word **information**.

6. When *Word* has finished searching the document a prompt appears, click **OK**. Close the **Find and Replace** dialog box.

7. With the cursor at the beginning of the text, find all occurrences of the word **text**. The word **information**, from the previous search, is highlighted in the **Find and Replace** dialog box. Type in the new word, **text**, to replace it.

8. Then use the **Find** feature to count how many times the word **record** appears in the document (check the **Answers** section). When the search is complete, a prompt will appear.

9. Click **OK** at the prompt and close the dialog box.

10. Save the document as **Defined** and leave it open for the following exercise.

Exercise 75 - Replacing Text

Guidelines:

From time to time it may be necessary to replace text in a document, e.g. if a name has changed. The **Replace** facility gives the option to exchange each occurrence of a particular word, or group of words, with an alternative.

Actions:

1. Use the document **Defined**. To replace the word **graphics** with **pictures**, click ⌗ Replace from the **Editing** group. This is the same dialog box as before, but with the **Replace** tab selected.

2. Enter **graphics** in the **Find what** box and **pictures** in **Replace with** box.

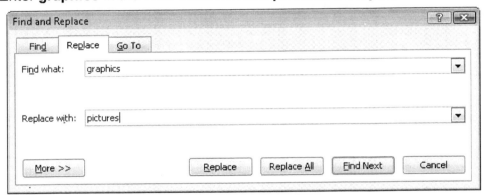

3. Select **Find Next** and click **Replace**.

Note: **Replace All** *will quickly replace all occurrences of the specified text.*

4. Continue through the document, replacing all occurrences of **graphics**. When the replacement is complete, a prompt will appear.

5. Click **OK** at the prompt. Close the **Find and Replace** dialog box.

6. Save the document and close it.

Note: *This feature can save time when typing a particular word or phrase repeatedly. Replace the word/phrase with* **#** *or a similar key press and, when the document is complete, use* **Find and Replace** *to change all occurrences of* **#**. *E.g.,* **DVLA** *could be replaced by* **Driving Vehicle Licensing Authority** *in this way.*

Exercise 76 - Word Count

Guidelines:

If you need to know how many words a document contains, the word count feature can be a useful tool. Document statistics such as number of pages, paragraphs, lines and characters can also be displayed.

Actions:

1. Open the document **Grand Canyon**.

2. Select the **Review** tab and click the **Word Count** button ![ABC 123] in the **Proofing** group. The **Document Statistics** can now be viewed.

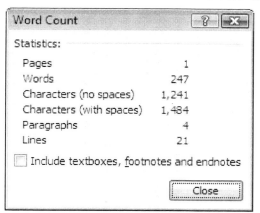

3. Click **Close**.

4. Look at the **Status Bar**. The number of words is shown there too.

Words: 247

5. Move to the end of the document and add a new line of text. Now look at the **Status Bar** to see that the number of words has increased.

6. Close the document <u>without</u> saving.

Exercise 77 - Revision

1.   Open the document **Errors**.

2.   Use any method to correct the spelling and grammar.

3.   Replace all occurrences of the word **Wendover** with **Sunderland**.

4.   Count the number of words in the document. How many words?

5.   **Print Preview** the document, print and then close it <u>without</u> saving.

Note: Check the **Answers** section at the end of the guide.

Exercise 78 - Revision

1.   Open the document **Grand Canyon**.

2.   **Replace** all instances of:

> **gorge** with **rocky gorge**
>
> **217** with **218**
>
> **1200** with **1300**
>
> **rarely** with **seldom**.

3.   Change the font of all the text to **Trebuchet MS**.

4.   Print the document.

5.   Close it <u>without</u> saving.

Exercise 79 - Revision

1.   Open **Grounds**.

2.   There are several spelling errors requiring correction. Do this now.

3.   There are probably one or two occasions where the suggestions made are insufficient. These must be corrected manually. You may need to refer to the note on Exercise 72. Correct the error(s) now.

4.   Print out the corrected document.

5.   Save the document as **Grounds3** and then close it.

Section 10

Formatting Paragraphs

By the end of the Section you should be able to:

Align Paragraphs

Change Line Spacing

Use Tabs and Indents

Insert Headers and Footers

Exercise 80 - Alignment

Guidelines:

Alignment refers to where text appears on each line in relation to the margins. There are four types of text alignment: **Left**, **Centred**, **Right** and **Justified** (full). Text is normally left aligned or justified (with straight left and right margins). Headings are often centred.

Note: In **Print Layout** view, alignment is shown as the cursor is moved across the page: I≡, I≣, ≡I . These special **Insertion Points** can be used before text is entered by clicking on the page and entering the text. Text will align according to which **Insertion Point** was used.

Actions:

1.   Open the document **Grand Canyon**.

2.   Use the <**Enter**> key to create a blank line at the start of the document.

3.   On the blank line, enter the title **The Grand Canyon** and make it bold.

4.   With the title still selected, click the **Center** button, [≣], in the **Paragraph** group, on the **Home** tab, to centre the title.

5.   Select the first paragraph. Click the **Justify** button, [≣]. Notice how the text now has straight right and left edges.

Note: When text is justified the spacing between words will change slightly. This is quite normal and does not need correction.

6.   Position the cursor within the second paragraph. Click the **Align Text Right** button, [≣]. As you can see, the paragraph does not need to be selected first, just place the cursor in the text and choose an alignment.

7.   Fully justify the remaining paragraphs.

8.   Print one copy of the document.

9.   Close the document <u>without</u> saving any changes.

Exercise 81 - Line Spacing

Guidelines:

The appearance of a document and the ease with which it may be read, can be improved by changing line spacing. By default, line spacing is **Single**; other commonly used spacing is **Double** and **1½**. Make sure you know what spacing is used where you work or study.

Actions:

1. Open the document **Dogs**.

2. Add your name to the bottom of the document.

3. Select all of the text, then click the **Line Spacing** button, 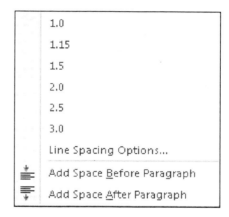, in the **Paragraph** group to display the line spacing options.

1.0
1.15
1.5
2.0
2.5
3.0
Line Spacing Options...
Add Space Before Paragraph
Add Space After Paragraph

4. Change the **Line Spacing** to **Double** by clicking **2.0**.

5. Justify the text. It is now much easier to read.

6. **Print Preview** the document.

7. Save the document as **Labs**.

8. Place the cursor at the beginning of the third sentence **The working dog...** and press <**Enter**> to create a new paragraph.

9. Select the new first paragraph and then change the spacing of the first paragraph to **1.5** lines.

10. Print out a copy of the amended document.

11. Try out other **Line Spacing** options.

12. Close the document <u>without</u> saving.

Exercise 82 - Using Tabs and Indents

Guidelines:

An indented paragraph is one where the text is further from the margin than the other paragraphs. The **<Tab>** key is used to indent just the first line of a paragraph (hanging paragraph), but the **Increase Indent** button, , on the toolbar is used to indent a whole paragraph. Each time the button is pressed, the paragraph is indented to the next tab stop (see page 114).

Actions:

1. Open the document **Grand Canyon**.

2. Fully justify the second paragraph.

3. Select the **Home** tab. Indent the third and fourth paragraphs to the first default tab stop by selecting them and using the **Increase Indent** button, , from the **Paragraph** group.

Note: *Press the **Indent** button as many times as necessary to indent the paragraph to the required tab stop.*

4. Place the insertion point in the third paragraph and press the **Decrease Indent** button, , to remove the indentation.

Note: *Increase Indent **<Ctrl M>**. Decrease Indent **<Ctrl Shift M>**.*

5. Place the cursor at the beginning of the first paragraph and indent the first line of the paragraph by pressing the **<Tab>** key.

6. Print a copy of the document to observe the effect of using indents and tabs.

7. Close the document <u>without</u> saving any changes.

Exercise 83 - Advanced Indentation

Guidelines:

Right, left and first line indent markers are displayed on the ruler. These enable the user to produce customised indents, without the need for re-setting the tabs.

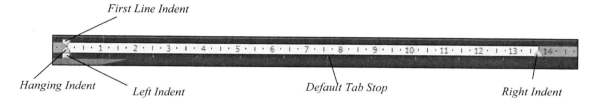

Actions:

1. Open **Grand Canyon** again.

2. Make sure the ruler is visible. If it is not, select the **View** tab and check the **Ruler** box in the **Show** group.

3. Position the cursor in the third paragraph.

4. Click and drag the first line indent marker (top triangle) on the left of the ruler, to **2 cm** on the ruler.

5. When the mouse button is released the first line of the paragraph will be indented to that position.

6. Now click and drag the hanging indent marker (lower triangle) on the left of the ruler to **1 cm**. When the mouse button is released the whole paragraph will be indented, except the first line which remains at **2 cm**.

7. Still in the same paragraph, indent the right side of the paragraph by selecting and dragging the triangle at the bottom right of the ruler to **12 cm**. When the mouse button is released the paragraph will be indented from the right.

8. Justify the paragraph.

9. Place the cursor at the beginning of the second paragraph and drag the **Left Indent** marker (the small square box) on the rule to **3 cm**. This action achieves the same result as repeatedly using the **Increase Indent** button on the **Ribbon**, but is more precise.

10. Now spend a few minutes experimenting.

11. Close **Grand Canyon** <u>without</u> saving.

Exercise 84 - Tabs

Guidelines:

Tabs are a precise measurement for aligning vertical rows of text in a document. Tab stops are set by default every **1.27 cm**. New tab settings will only apply to text that has been selected, or is yet to be typed. Tab settings are displayed on the ruler.

Actions:

1.   Start a new document. On the **Page Layout** tab, click the **Paragraph** dialog box launcher and click **Tabs** button to display the **Tabs** dialog box.

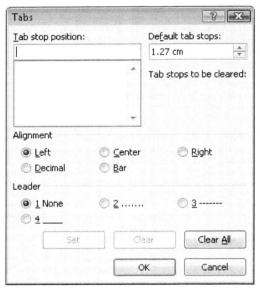

2.   Enter **1 cm** in the **Tab stop position** box. Check the **Alignment** is **Left** and the **Leader** is **None**. Click **Set** to set the first tab.

3.   Now enter **10** in the **Tab stop position box**, (cm is assumed if omitted). Click **Set**, then click **OK**.

4.   Notice an **L** marker has appeared on the ruler; this indicates the chosen setting. Press the <**Tab**> key before typing the word **Salesperson** and press <**Tab**> again to move to the next tab setting. Type **Sales** and press <**Enter**> to move to the next line. Enter the following information using the same method.

J Heslop	**126.56**
M Fisher	**56**
K Lowe	**340.75**
D Green	**9.5**
S Evans	**1200**
A Hargreaves	**50.98**

continued over

Exercise 84 - Continued

5.   Save the document as **Tabs** and print a copy.

Note: *To quickly set tabs, click at the required position on the ruler. A tab symbol will appear where it is set.*

6.   Now select the entire document, display the **Tabs** dialog box and select **Clear All**. Click **OK**. This will remove all the manually set tab stops and the tab controls in the text will line up to the default tab stops.

7.   With the entire document selected, use the mouse to click on the ruler at approximately **0.5 cm** and **7 cm** to set tabs. The text will now line up with the new tab stops.

Note: *Additional tab stops can be set by clicking on the required position on the ruler.*

8.   Print a copy of the document and close it <u>without</u> saving the changes.

9.   Open the file **Contents List**. Select the whole document and display the **Tabs** dialog box.

10.   The two columns are too far apart. Before the tabs can be changed, select **Clear All** to remove the original tabs.

Note: *Tabs can be removed by clicking on them and dragging the tab markers down, off the ruler.*

11.   Set a new tab by entering **4 cm** in the **Tab stop position** box. Click on **Set**.

12.   Repeat this for a tab at **11 cm**. Click **OK**. View the changes.

Note: *Tab positions can be changed by clicking and dragging the tab along the ruler to the required position.*

13.   With the document still selected, click on the left tab marker at **4 cm** on the ruler and drag to **5 cm**. Release the mouse button. The first column will move.

14.   Click on the first tab marker and drag it down off the ruler. The text automatically shifts to the next tab marker.

15.   Create a new tab stop at **3 cm**.

16.   Practise using the mouse and ruler to move and remove tab markers.

17.   Close the document <u>without</u> saving.

Exercise 85 - Headers and Footers

Guidelines:

Headers and **Footers** are common identification lines at the top and/or bottom of each page. When such text is found at the top of a page it is called a header; those at the bottom are termed footers. Different headers and footers can be placed on alternate pages, or the same header/footer on every page.

Actions:

1. Open the document **Sharks**. Delete all lines above the first main paragraph of text.

2. Select the **Insert** tab and click **Header**, then click **Edit Header**. The header area at the top of the page is made active.

Note: *Double clicking in the blank area at the top of a page will also activate the header.*

3. The **Design** tab should be displayed. Look in the **Options** group, and make sure that neither **Different First Page** nor **Different Odd & Even Pages** is checked.

4. In the header area, press <**Tab**> type **Sharks**, press <**Enter**> and press <**Tab**> and type **By A. Fule**. This is then a two line header.

5. Click **Go to Footer**, to switch to the **Footer**.

6. Click the **Quick Parts** button and select **Field**. In the **Field** dialog box, scroll down the list of **Field Names** and select **FileName**. Click **OK** to insert the automatic field at the left of the footer.

7. Press <**Tab**>. Click **Date and Time**, and click **OK** to insert the date in the centre of the footer with the default date format.

8. To close the **Footer**, click **Close Header and Footer**. The main document is active again.

9. **Print Preview** to view the header and footer.

10. Print a copy of the document, then close it <u>without</u> saving.

Note: ***Headers and Footers** are only visible in **Print Layout View** or **Print Preview**.*

Exercise 86 - Revision

1.   Open the document **Chuffington Hall**.

2.   Add a centred title, **Theft**. Change the font size to **16pt** and make it **bold**.

3.   Centre the first paragraph.

4.   Justify the second paragraph.

5.   Right align the third paragraph.

6.   Print the document and close it <u>without</u> saving.

Exercise 87 - Revision

1.   Open the document **Company Info**.

2.   Italicise all instances of **CiA Training Ltd**.

3.   **Center** all of the text in the document.

4.   Select all of the text and change the line spacing to **1.5** lines.

5.   Print a copy.

6.   Close **Company Info** <u>without</u> saving.

Exercise 88 - Revision

1.   Open the document **Applications**.

2.   Justify all of the text.

3.   Apply a hanging indent at **2 cm** to each paragraph.

4.   Insert a header and type your name in the centre of it.

5.   Use a button on the Ribbon to enter today's date at the left of the footer.

6.   Remove all indentation from the text.

7.   Select the whole document and create a tab at **2.5 cm**. Tab the first line of each paragraph to the new tab stop.

8.   Save the file as **Applications2** and close it.

Exercise 89 - Revision

1.   Open the document **Business Letter**.

2.   First you will notice the spelling and grammar mistakes. Correct them now.

3.   Select the address at the top of the page. Right align it. Underline the words in the address.

4.   Select the remainder of the letter and fully justify it.

5.   Change the font for the entire letter to **Arial 11pt Italic**.

6.   Select each of the sub headings and make them **12pt** and **bold**. Centre each of them.

7.   Remove the sentence containing **24/7**.

8.   Change the margins to top **4.5**, right and left **1.5 cm**.

9.   Replace all occurrences of **Europe** with **The World**.

10.   Select the heading **Will it benefit my company?** and its associated paragraph. Delete it.

11.   Select each of the paragraphs under the sub headings and make the line spacing **1.5** lines.

12.   Move the heading and associated paragraph **What will it cost?** to follow **Why should you choose us?**. Adjust any spacing to match the rest of the letter.

13.   Preview the document and print a copy.

14.   Save the document as **My letter**.

15.   Close the document.

16.   Open **Business Letter Complete** and print it out. This is what your document should look like. Compare the two. Check for any differences. If there are any, find out why yours is different and make the necessary changes to your letter.

17.   Close all open documents.

18.   Exit *Word*.

Answers

Exercise 13

Step 1   The **keyboard** is used to type information.

Step 2   The term for parts of a computer is **hardware**.

Step 3   The programs used on the computer are known as **software**.

Step 4   Working without regular breaks can cause eye strain.

Step 5   **Repetitive Strain Injury** can be caused by poor posture and repeating the same movements over a long time.

Step 6   You may have to use a password to log on to the computer.

Step 7   Icons are pictures representing items on the computer.

Step 8   The pointer means the computer is busy.

Step 9   The **Start** menu is displayed by clicking the **Start** button.

Step 10   Click the small arrow and select **Shut down** from the menu.

Exercise 21

Step 1   An icon appears on the **Taskbar** to represent each open window.

Exercise 32

Step 7   The folder contains **2** other folders, a **Word 2007 data** folder and the **Exercises** folder.

Exercise 33

Step 7

Step 9

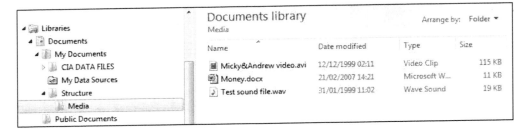

Exercise 45

Step 2 There are **2** methods of opening a file in *Word*: clicking **Open** after clicking the **Office Button**, or using the list of recently opened files at the right of the **Office** menu.

Step 3 You will need to click the **Office Button**.

Step 4 There are usually **17** documents listed to the right of the menu.

Step 6 The **View** buttons are located at the **right** of the **Status Bar**.

Step 7 **No**, the document is unchanged, you are just viewing it differently.

Step 10 The **New** button is available after clicking the **Office Button** and has a blank page on it with the corner turned down. Either double click the **Blank Document** icon or click the **Create** button with the **Blank Document** selected.

Exercise 49

Step 2 The button can be dragged **down** to view the bottom of the page or you can click within the **Scroll Bar** below the scroll button.

Step 3 **<Ctrl End>** will place the Insertion point at the end of the document.

Exercise 74

Step 8 The word **record** appears **3** times in the document (twice within **records**).

Exercise 77

Step 4 335 words in the document.

Glossary

Alignment	The position of the text on the page in relation to the margins.
Backspace key	A key that moves the cursor to the left, erasing any characters in its path. This should not be confused with the **Delete** key.
Character	Any letter, number or symbol typed in, even a space.
Clipboard	An area of temporary storage memory, used when cutting or copying.
Computer	A folder available in all versions of *Windows*, which is the default location for storing user data.
Delete key	A key on the keyboard that erases any text that is selected, or is to the right of the cursor. This should not be confused with the **Backspace** key.
Document	Any file created in *Word*, it can have one or many pages.
Drag and Drop	A technique for moving selected text from one position to another.
Edit	To make changes to existing text.
File Extension	3 or 4 characters following every file name, which define what type of file it is and also what application will be used by default to open it.
Navigation pane	Part of the *Windows Explorer* window showing a structured list of libraries and folders.
Font	A type or style of print.
Icon	Small picture representing an object such as a file, folder, or program.
Insertion Point	The place on the page where the cursor flashes.
Justify	To align text so that both left and right margins are straight.
Multiple Selection	Selecting several files and/or folders from a display so that an action can be applied to all of them.
Point	A measurement of the size of text. 1 point = 1/72 of an inch.
Print Preview	A feature that shows how a document will look before it is printed.

continued over

Recycle Bin	An area of storage where deleted files are held temporarily before being deleted completely.
Save	To keep a copy of a file on a storage disk.
Selection Bar	An invisible area at the left of the page, used to select rows of text.
Shortcut	An icon (usually found on the **Desktop** area) which opens an application, file or folder stored elsewhere.
Subfolder	A folder that is contained within another folder.
Symbol	A character which can be used in text but is not normally found on the keyboard.
Tab	A way of lining up items in a list of text.
Taskbar	By default, a bar running the length of the **Desktop**, at the bottom of the screen. Shows which tasks the computer is performing.
View	The layout of a page as displayed on the screen; e.g. **Print Layout**, **Draft**, etc.
Word Processor	An application for the creation and manipulation of text documents.
Word Wrap	How the computer automatically detects the end of a line and starts a new one.
WYSIWYG	An acronym describing the type of screen layout displayed by a word processor running under *Windows*: What you see is what you get.
Zoom	A feature that either allows the document to be viewed more closely, or more of the document to be viewed, but in less detail.

Index

Record of Achievement Matrix

This Matrix is to be used to measure your progress while working through the guide. This is a self assessment process, you judge when you are competent. Remember that afterwards there is an assessment to test your competence.

Tick boxes are provided for each feature. 1 is for no knowledge, 2 is for some knowledge and 3 is for competent. A section is only complete when column 3 is completed for all parts of the section.

Tick the Relevant Boxes **1**: No Knowledge **2**: Some Knowledge **3**: Competent

Section	No	Exercise	1	2	3
1 Fundamentals	1	Introduction to your Computer			
	2	Health and Safety			
	3	Security			
	4	Logging On			
	5	The Windows Desktop			
	6	The Mouse: Holding and Moving			
	7	The Mouse: Clicking			
	8	The Mouse: Dragging			
	9	Mouse Pointers			
	10	The Taskbar			
	11	The Start Menu			
	12	Shut Down and Restart the Computer			
2 Windows	14	About Windows			
	15	Opening Windows			
	16	Closing Windows			
	17	Resizing and Moving Windows			
	18	Scroll Bars			
	19	Dialog Boxes			
	20	Changing Basic Settings			
3 File Management	22	Understanding Files and Folders			
	23	Views			
	24	Creating a New Folder			
	25	Moving Files and Folders			
	26	Copying Files and Folders			
	27	Selecting Multiple Files			
	28	Renaming Files and Folders			
	29	Deleting Files and Folders			
	30	The Recycle Bin			
	31	Printing File Structure			
4 Introduction to Word Processing	34	Starting Word			
	35	The Layout of the Word Screen			
	36	Exiting Word			

Other Products from CiA Training

CiA Training is a leading publishing company, which has consistently delivered the highest quality products since 1985. A wide range of flexible and easy to use self teach resources has been developed by CiA's experienced publishing team to aid the learning process. These include the following materials at the time of publication of this product:

- **Open Learning Guides**

- **ECDL/ICDL & ECDL/ICDL Advanced (ECDL Foundation Qualification)**

- **New CLAIT, CLAIT Plus & CLAIT Advanced (OCR Qualification)**

- **CiA Revision Series**

- **ITQs (Industry Standard Qualification)**

- **e-Citizen (ECDL Foundation Qualification)**

- **Trainer's Packs with iCourse**

- **Start IT (City & Guilds Qualification)**

- **Skill for Life in ICT (Industry Standard Qualification)**

- **iCourse - Course customising software**

We hope you have enjoyed using our materials and would love to hear your opinions about them. If you'd like to give us some feedback, please go to:

www.ciatraining.co.uk/feedback.php

and let us know what you think.

New products are constantly being developed. For up to the minute information on our products, to view our full range, to find out more, or to be added to our mailing list, visit:

www.ciatraining.co.uk